Building a Garage

A COMPLETE GUIDE

Building a Garage

A COMPLETE GUIDE

Laurie Williamson

THE CROWOOD PRESS

First published in 2011 by
The Crowood Press Ltd
Ramsbury, Marlborough
Wiltshire SN8 2HR

www.crowood.com

British Library Cataloguing-in-Publication Data
A catalogue record for this book is available from the British Library.

ISBN 978 1 84797 222 4

Disclaimer
The author and the publisher do not accept any responsibility, in any
manner whatsoever, for any error, or omission, nor any loss, damage,
injury, adverse outcome or liability of any kind incurred as a result of
the use of any of the information contained in this book, or reliance
upon it. Readers are advised to seek professional advice relating to their
particular garage, house, project and circumstances before embarking on
any building or installation work.

Photographic Acknowledgements
The author and the publishers are grateful to the following individuals,
manufacturers and businesses who have very kindly provided
photographs that appear in this book: Mark Channen of Boddingtons
Ltd, Grass Reinforcement Solutions; Broadoak Buildings; Martyn Phillips
of The BRP Group (Cardale Doors, Henderson Garage Doors, Wessex
Doors and Steel-Line Security Products); Neil O'Sullivan of Compton
Buildings (0800 9758860, www.comptonbuildings.co.uk); Simon
Hendriksen of Crown Buildings Ltd; Kathryn Lee of Gliderol Garage
Doors Ltd and David Glen Walker; Chris Praat of Mech-Mate Motor Pits
Ltd; and Walker E. Hamilton of Oakmasters.

Cover photos courtesy Boddingtons Grass Reinforcement Solutions,
Compton Garages, Gliderol Garage Doors, Henderson Garage Doors,
Mech-Mate Motorpits and the author.

Typeset by Servis Filmsetting Ltd, Stockport, Cheshire
Printed and bound in Malaysia by Times Offset (M) Sdn Bhd

Contents

Introduction

Always high on the list of priorities placed upon today's developer is the consideration 'How best can I utilize the space available?' Planners and designers have always tried to keep pace with the rapid changes created by modern society, but this is an almost impossible assignment. A clear area of dissatisfaction concerns the current multi-vehicle ownership family, whose demands are at odds with the rapidly reducing area designated per property for development, and the environment strains being faced globally. Add to this the close proxim-ity of each property to its neighbour, and at times there is an unbearable strain on the space available for parking and mobility activity. One solution would be to increase the hectareage used per dwelling, but with land prices at such a premium this is extremely unlikely to be approved.

The solution must lie in the best utilization of the space available, while considering the 'long term' view. Sometimes there is no possibility of building a garage at all because there is no space available; and for many home owners a new garage

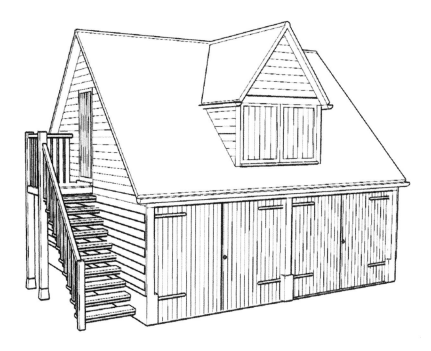

has already been built as a 'permanent' domestic structure, rather than their selecting one of the many temporary demountable structures available in the market place. Evidence of this is substantiated by the steady increase in local authority building construction applications.

The reasons for this steady increase are economic as well as aesthetic, and, supported by the ready availability of both the materials and the experienced labour required to carry out everyday domestic construction projects successfully, developers have become emboldened however small in scale the project is.

However, 'caution' must always be the byword where any construction project is being considered, and this increase does not mean that the process is easy. A garage as an individual, stand-alone building project is a very specific building, with structural requirements that are many and varied – but it is its location that attracts the most attention. Accessibility to both the highway and the existing dwelling will need to be considered, and it is essential to esnure that the garage can be used with ease and safety. Another important factor will be how the new building will blend in with any existing buildings.

Building a Garage is a step-by-step illustrated guide designed to assist anyone who is planning such a building project. From initial conception through to final completion, every aspect has been considered, with an in-depth review of design and construction. You will be required to consider what you are trying to achieve, and what the building structure is to be used for: simply as a comfortable home for a prized motor vehicle, or for additional storage, as an extended workspace, or where home amenities can be used. The choices are many and varied.

The construction method itself will also need to be considered. Maybe you have both the time and the expertise to carry out the work yourself, or you may need to involve experienced contractors to carry out part or all of the work for you. *Building a Garage* is ideal for home owners and DIY enthusiasts alike, includes points of good building practice to be observed during the construction process and offers guidance when organizing and assisting builders and contractors.

CHAPTER 1

Selecting a Garage

Building a new garage is potentially a project with a huge array of possibilities within its remit: it can be wide ranging in complexity, or indeed extremely simple, and relatively easy for a competent do-it-yourself enthusiast to complete successfully on his own.

A VARIETY OF DESIGNS

The designs for such a project are many and varied, ranging from a single, basic storage compartment for one vehicle of indeterminate size, to a majestic multi-use construction that serves the needs of a variety of domestic and fitness ambitions; it may be of single or double wall thickness, and there is a huge choice of materials it can be made of. Those regularly used include pre-cast concrete slabs slotted together according to prepared plans, softwood and hardwood timber creating a barn-like structure in a whole variety of designs, and the standard brick and block construction used so widely in general domestic situations.

Two-bay, oak-framed garage.

Two-bay, oak-framed garage with room over.

Oak-framed garages are proving extremely popular nowadays, and there is an extensive range of design possibilities, from bespoke hand-made components through to ready-to-assemble kits for the experienced DIY builder. Oak has been used as a traditional building material for centuries, and has truly passed the test of time. Magnificent purpose-built oak-framed garages built from sustainable woodland are now available in a range of styles that will meet almost every need. Centuries-old carpentry skills used on home-grown 'green' building materials, and benefiting from modern techniques, produce an end result of elegance and beauty with the potential for a very long life.

For the dedicated self-build enthusiast working within fixed parameters, an ideal and practical solution may be found in the portable or demountable garage market. For several decades portable garage manufacturers have provided an ever-improving and increasing range of designs and styles to meet the need for a state-of-the-art, weatherproof solution to vehicle storage and protection without having to pay too much. The ranges currently available from a large number of experienced suppliers offer an extensive choice with something to suit every pocket – a comprehensive variety of styles, sizes and shapes including traditional and modern designs all produced using only the highest quality materials.

The benefits or differences between erecting a portable garage and a permanent one are many and varied. The one shared point will be the base upon which the garage is built. A secure level concrete base is recommended, and any guarantees provided by the garage manufacturers will depend upon how well the base is laid and how level it is. The quality of the base material may well also determine how the new garage works and what maintenance is required during its lifetime.

With such a variety of roof styles and wall finishes available, the appearance of the new garage can be selected from the wide range available. Single and double doors can be fitted, along with windows and entrance doors. The majority of manufacturers will provide a supply and build service on the base you have built.

Inspection pit.

When you have selected the garage to suit your particular needs, then other factors need to be looked at before pen is put to paper. The appearance of this new structure is singularly important, so it is essential to choose the garage door you prefer before the plans have been prepared. The style, function and operating room required must all be decided at an early stage. With so many garage doors available 'off the peg', these dimensions should be included on the building plans. Custom-made doors can be produced where aperture sizes do not meet the standard sizes available, but these doors will be more expensive, and ordering time must be allowed to prevent delays on the build.

And finally, issues relating to what the garage is to be used for, and the effect it will have on the surrounding area, will need to be addressed. If it is to be used for repairs besides just storage of a motor vehicle, then an inspection pit built in during the construction process may be a welcome addition. Working on your car is much easier with an inspection pit in your garage: think of all the jobs where you have to crawl about underneath it – oil changes, exhaust swaps, greasing, welding – all fairly unpleasant. An inspection pit makes access to the underside of your car easy, allowing you to work in well lit comfort with all your tools to hand.

The Driveway

Concerning the area surrounding the new garage, we need to look at the driveway and consider how, by using eco-friendly 'green' products, we can relieve any pressures on the local 'climate' and water table; all are guaranteed to meet the general design requirements. With so much news based on climate change and global warming, there is also a drive to prevent, or at least defer, the effects of this phenomenon, particularly where savings can be made. Practically speaking, an eco-friendly driveway should be easy to install and attractive to look at, and can be very cost effective, although it is likely to need regular maintenance.

An eco-friendly driveway.

Such a driveway can be constructed using driveway honeycomb grids made from recycled plastic with the cells filled with a mixture of sand and soil. The area is then seeded and treated, as with a standard lawn.

Why a Garage?

Before making even the most basic of decisions with regard to design, the first question to address is 'Why do we need a garage?' It may be required to provide adequate protection from inclement

Shingle driveway.

or adverse weather conditions, where anything from a lean-to structure or even a car port may meet with immediate requirements. Alternatively, where the vehicle in question needs to be stored, even for very short periods, in a building that is absolutely secure, then the design and build will need to be far more complex and demanding.

Once this question is fully answered, then you will know more exactly the type of structure that needs to be designed and built. It is fairly safe to say that every possible design will have been considered at some time during the life of the current motor vehicle, and every type of construction. However, although the object of this

Attached flat-roof garage.

Attached lean-to garage.

attention has changed over the decades, it will be only in the minor matter of size: otherwise not much has changed at all. Uses other than those of storage will be dealt with at a later stage; in the meantime, storage, assembly and repair are all avenues to be considered before plans are drawn up.

When the full use of this new building has been determined, then design and location need to be addressed. As mentioned earlier, design will certainly have been extensively researched, with many books and magazines promoting different designs available on the internet or in the local library. If you can't find anything to satisfy your requirements, then design professionals are available promoting almost every shape and size. Taking any design to extremes, however, may well fall foul of planning rules, so anything considered out of the ordinary is best brought before the local authority planning officers before pen is put to paper in anger.

THE SINGLE GARAGE

Most common of all is the 'single' garage, designed and built to accommodate just one average-sized family car, with little room for anything else. However, as vehicles have grown in size in recent years, existing garages – those built, say, twenty years ago – have become difficult to use, with the car occupant often having to squeeze in and out of the car door, so restricted has the space become between the vehicle and the garage wall, the direct result of the increase in vehicle width during the

Single-section garage.

Attached single garage.

last two decades. It was also not unusual to see a car occupant getting out of the car in front of the garage and actually pushing it in – and of course a similar procedure was required to get it out. Nevertheless, although future changes in vehicle shape and size may only be surmised, it is likely that vehicles will reduce in size over the next few decades, rather than increase.

The internal measurements for a standard single garage are 2.4 by 4.8m (8 by 15.7ft), or 11.5sq m (125sq ft), but these dimensions are not likely to accommodate an oversized vehicle, nor will they allow you to move comfortably around even the average-sized car. Where there is a requirement to work on, or carry out repairs to the vehicle, or to move around it comfortably, or where additional space is needed for whatever reason, then any plans will need to make allowance for this. Of course the dimensions above are based on standard measurements, and may not be suitable where the garage needs to allow for these or any other extraordinary circumstances.

THE DOUBLE GARAGE

Double garage.

Double garage with room in roof.

Double-section garage.

Next up the scale from a single garage is the double garage, designed to store two cars either alongside each other or one behind the other. A double garage can also vary significantly in size and design, and can have one or two garage doors on the front elevation. Of course a larger area of ground will be required for this particular project, and there will be more emphasis on structural stability. However, the access required for a double garage would not need to be larger than for a single garage. The approximate internal dimensions of a double garage would be 4.9 by 4.8m (16 by 15.7ft), covering a ground area of 23.5sq m (251sq ft). These dimensions are for guidance purposes only and are based upon a standard double-garage door with sufficient side piers to provide a strong and stable structure and enough depth to accept a standard family car.

MULTIPLE GARAGES

It is fair to say that single and double garages fill the largest quotient of garage-building projects, but further multiples are not uncommon. Such is the current ownership of motor vehicles and their intrinsic value, more buildings of a larger size, with room for three and four vehicles, occur on the planning application lists and are clearly for private and domestic use as opposed to commercial.

Thus it is not uncommon for garages to be built in larger multiples than single and double; however, although the construction period and preparations follow the same designated pattern, larger garage sizes are determined by the land available. Furthermore, subject to sufficient land being available and a thorough exploration of access facilities and road traffic considerations, larger and more complex garage proposals would, inevitably, need to meet the requirements of the local authority planning department.

Row of garages. Multiple garages are not uncommon, even for private use.

CHAPTER 2

Getting Started

Adding to, extending, improving, updating, remodelling and converting properties has of late become the norm almost to the exclusion of all other activities. What was once an activity singularly driven by a buoyant and flourishing home housing market, this very British occupation and pastime has now become more and more popular, even in areas not previously noted for their extensive building activity. Of course, originally the number of ageing properties requiring improvement seemed infinite, and the drive to bring them in line with twentieth and twenty-first century requirements unquenched – but then as the demand grew and the number of properties with potential decreased, the boundaries were raised.

Popularized, in many cases, by television programmes highlighting the benefits to be gained by the experienced and the novice builder alike, whatever the condition or location, it now seems that no country within the European Community has escaped the headlong drive towards improvement. This cannot be a bad thing in itself, but it shows no immediate signs of abating, and while the demand for land and property is so intense the true value of the range of property improvements available may be dissembled.

The addition of a new garage falls neatly within this incentive, and within many other schemes under consideration, or in plans to improve an existing property for both practical and financial benefits; this might also include the conversion of a barn or outbuilding to be used as a garage. Such a project can be readily included within the set parameters of the existing property; it can be of simple or more characterful design, and accommodated within an existing layout.

Planning Permission

You will need planning permission to construct a new garage if it falls within any one of the following parameters:

- It is within 5m of the existing house.
- It is to be positioned in front of the building line, nearer the highway than any part of the original house.
- The height at the eaves exceeds 2.5m and 4m at the ridge.
- If it is within 2m of a boundary, and the eaves' height exceeds 2.5m.
- Where more than half of the land around the original house is occupied by additions or other buildings.
- When the garage is to be used for business.
- Where the property lies within a national park.

To ensure that building work is carried out in compliance with local authority planning rules, discuss your plans with the local planning officer.

When contemplating the building of a new garage it is important to recognize that there is no 'one size fits all' solution. In some areas a

Building along the boundary.

new garage can be viewed as an extremely valuable asset, whereas in others a more appropriate course of action would be additional living space. It is, however, a relevant fact that where several vehicles are owned per household, insurance companies increasingly insist that secure garaging is provided in order to reduce vehicle insurance premiums – and in this case a new garage can pay for itself in only a few years. This can be more important in areas where parking 'off road' is extremely limited or insecure, front gardens are almost non-existent, and where secure vehicle storage is a necessity and adds value and saleability to a house.

In some, mainly urban areas, to use available and valuable garden space to build a new garage may be questionable; but in the majority of mainly rural areas around the country, this is quite acceptable.

In reality the reason for this work may have nothing to do with property values, but is simply to add to the existing accommodation in response to the needs of a growing family. Of course these new additions may not be limited to one proposal and one outcome, and could be designed to include and provide an annexe for an elderly relative – or they may just be to add extra footage to the existing 'living' area. Whatever the reason, the work should be carried out to complement the existing property while remaining within the requirements stipulated by local planning and building regulations.

Building Regulations

The new garage will require building regulations approval if it falls within one of the following parameters:

- The floor area exceeds 30sq m.
- The new garage is to be built within 1m of a boundary.
- The garage is constructed from bricks, blocks, tiles and so on.
- The new garage is attached to the existing house.

To check if your new garage requires building regulations approval, contact your local authority building control officer.

*Detached garage built along
the boundary.*

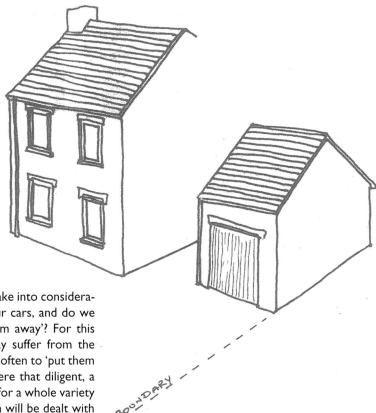

BOUNDARY

Another important point to take into consideration is how often do we use our cars, and do we really need a space to 'put them away'? For this reason the garage of today may suffer from the fact that we use our cars far too often to 'put them away' every time. Even if we were that diligent, a garage can by necessity be used for a whole variety of other activities, each of which will be dealt with during the course of this book.

Size is important. In the recent past garages were designed and built in huge numbers to accommodate the smaller range of cars in manufacture, not for the 'people carriers' and four-wheel-drive vehicles currently frequenting our roads. Not that a new garage should be built to cope with these hybrids, nevertheless a careful projection of where the current car market is heading will help when decisions are made regarding size and location.

Added to this equation is the steep rise in house prices in recent years. With the whole process of moving home becoming more and more expensive, utilizing the existing facilities and improving them may be a better 'value for money' alternative.

All these are 'plus' points – and yet there are still more. A garage is generally a simple construction requiring a modest outlay against return; it can be attached to the side of the house, or be an integral part of the front elevation. The walls, floor, founda-tions and roof can also be used to provide additional living accommodation within the main structure; this can be simple in plan and straightforward to execute. Where the garage is located close to or against the side of the existing dwelling, this new space can be used as, for example, an extension to the existing kitchen, or even a new dining room; another common use is a self-contained 'annexe' for an elderly relative requiring independent access.

By adding a new construction the range of possibilities for improvement is hugely increased, many of which will be considered and covered in some detail during the stages of this book. For these reasons a new garage is now seen to be an asset, and far too expensive a construction to be used simply as a storeroom, where bicycles, running machines, chest freezers and workbenches gather dust. It is a dry, weatherproof area where plans for fitness regimes and the production of

Integral garage.

Attached and integral garage.

To reduce the possibility of reversing onto a highway, you will have to provide a suitable vehicle turning area adjacent to the new garage.

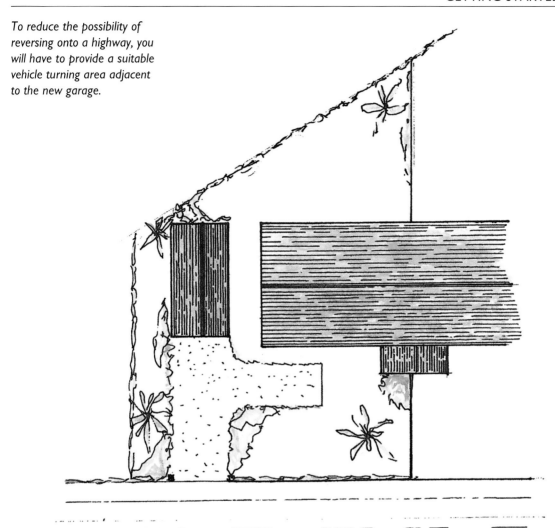

do-it-yourself furniture can be nurtured with intensity – even if in reality they are highly unlikely to be fulfilled. Now the garage is rapidly regaining its identity within its original format, with more and more being included in the 'living space' agenda.

As with any building project, however large or small, success or failure will lie in the planning – and planning covers all aspects of the work, from start to completion. Decisions must be made and finalized, and advice, when required, must be sought. Expensive mistakes and costly errors lie in wait for the unprepared and inexperienced.

To start with, the viability of a new build or a conversion, and which to go for, should be addressed. What space is available 'on the ground'? What best will be achieved with either a new build or a conversion? How much will it cost? And will it have the desired effect? This may be a DIY project, or if the work is complicated, it may require the extensive use of qualified sub-contract workers. With such a wide range of decisions to be made, making plans and where possible sticking to them is often the key to complete success.

21

*Where more than
one vehicle is in use,
provision for a 'passing'
space is advisable.*

SITE SURVEY

Before any money is spent and any firm decisions made, it is important to size up the area for suitability. Not all garages will work well within the existing boundaries and surrounding properties; access may be limited or even unavailable, and not to plan well could result in a project that proves to be a total waste of time and money.

Perhaps the plan is to build the garage directly adjacent to the existing structure or dwelling, and therefore limit the number of structural alterations and layout variables currently available on site. Alternatively it may be to make the maximum possible use of the space available, even taking into consideration how the new work can be maximized with, for example, a possible future plan for building above the new garage. Whatever the considerations, whatever the hopes and plans, it would be wise, initially, to carry out a simple site survey to determine all the possibilities and prepare for any future additions that may come to fruition.

This initial and indeed crucial part of the planning process should be carried out by an architect or someone with similar expertise well before any firm plans are prepared, and also to determine any building control requirements that must be addressed. The problem with this approach if there is a problem, is that proposed development works are likely to be dictated by the nature and shape of the existing structure, thus limiting the hitherto large range of possibilities. Of course the very first considerations must be given to what you would like to achieve. Will you be able to end up with exactly what you want, and will it compliment the existing structure should your requirements be met? By starting from this semi-neutral position the proposed project can be viewed overall by what the end result will be, and not by the position you started from.

Where possible, of course, it would be wise to familiarize yourself with a few of the more important building and planning requirements this

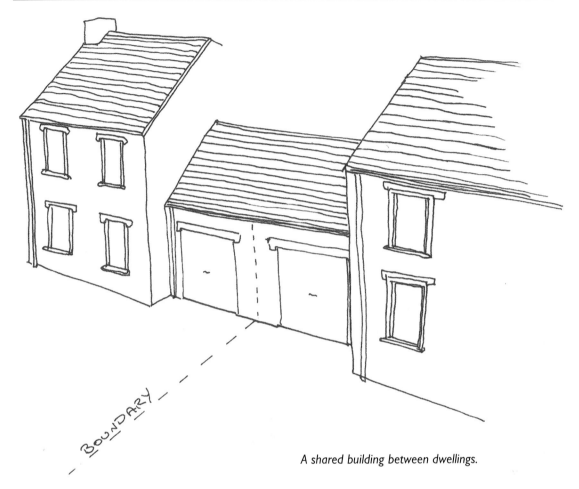

BOUNDARY

A shared building between dwellings.

type of development would have to meet – points that may inevitably mean that it cannot possibly be viable, that may push both the building and financial boundaries just that bit too far. These very important points will include existing ground levels, existing and proposed drainage positions, roof levels and the proposed roof structure. If you find that these points can be dealt with easily, then I am sure any sensible requirements planned within the existing boundaries can be achieved and may be viewed with a positive consideration. It is at this stage, after you have decided loosely what you want to get out of the new development, that an architect or draughtsman should be approached with a view to feasibility discussions, and then hopefully the preparation of the building plans.

To start with we will therefore look at each of these important points, first individually and then as a group.

Position

The first consideration, and this will seem fairly obvious, will be how the garage will be positioned, and whether or not the proposals indicate that it will blend in with the existing property. Similar garages around the area may already have been constructed, so ideas can be gleaned from the experience of others. Where this is not the case, then you will have to decide what you want to achieve while looking at both the front and also the rear elevation. The plan may include a whole range of garage doors from standard to specialized; alternatively it may be positioned and

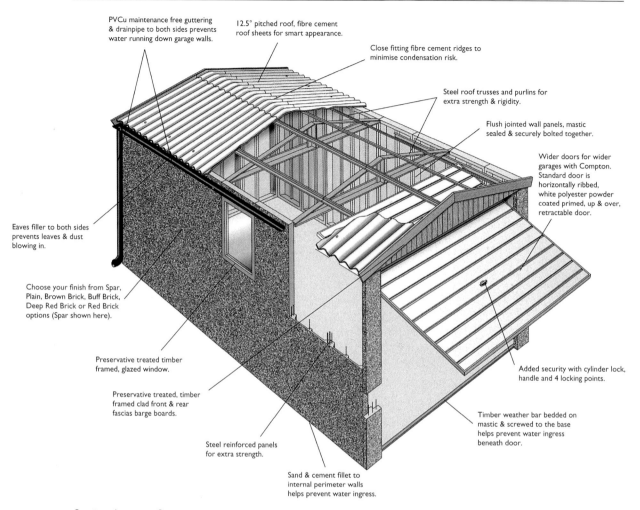

PVCu maintenance free guttering & drainpipe to both sides prevents water running down garage walls.

12.5° pitched roof, fibre cement roof sheets for smart appearance.

Close fitting fibre cement ridges to minimise condensation risk.

Steel roof trusses and purlins for extra strength & rigidity.

Flush jointed wall panels, mastic sealed & securely bolted together.

Wider doors for wider garages with Compton. Standard door is horizontally ribbed, white polyester powder coated primed, up & over, retractable door.

Eaves filler to both sides prevents leaves & dust blowing in.

Choose your finish from Spar, Plain, Brown Brick, Buff Brick, Deep Red Brick or Red Brick options (Spar shown here).

Preservative treated timber framed, glazed window.

Preservative treated, timber framed clad front & rear fascias barge boards.

Added security with cylinder lock, handle and 4 locking points.

Timber weather bar bedded on mastic & screwed to the base helps prevent water ingress beneath door.

Steel reinforced panels for extra strength.

Sand & cement fillet to internal perimeter walls helps prevent water ingress.

Sectional garage features.

designed to compliment the existing entrance door or doors.

An important point of the construction work from both a design and an aesthetics point of view, will be the position of the lintel over the new garage door. It is likely that plans will be required to show that this lintel is horizontally in line with other lintels on the property, and this point will be duplicated where a window or windows and any other doors are involved. If the lintel over the garage door is likely to be higher or lower than the other lintels on the property, then some planning work may be required to balance these visible effects; it may be necessary to raise, lower or even replace the lintel.

Ground Levels

A second important factor to take into consideration will be the existing ground levels. It is quite normal for the garage floor level to be lower than the existing house floor level, though simply raising this level may not be the answer. On a level site planning the positioning and layout will be straightforward, but where the site is sloping or dramatically uneven the layout may require some work. Levelling the site could be a possibility, but in many instances this may not be viable. Where the layout obviously requires outside expertise, then the employment of an architect may prove to be extremely beneficial.

Up-and-over garage door.

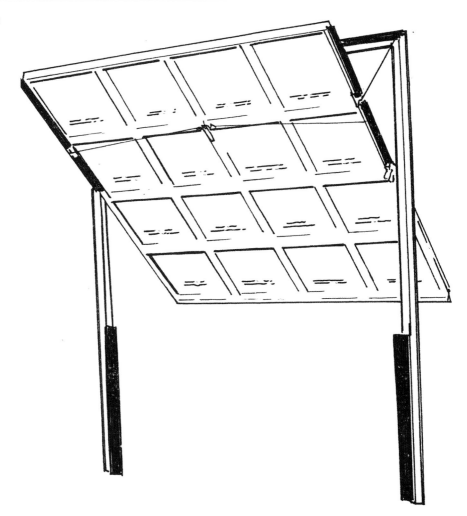

The Roof Level

A third and equally important survey point is the proposed roof level: is the new structure set at the correct level, and what effect, if any, will this have on the existing or neighbouring roof levels? The design and structure will need to compliment the existing buildings, and should be checked for suitability when the building plans are prepared.

Mains Services

Finally, every new development on an existing site will be affected by the location of the mains services, and these may well play a significant role in the positioning of any planned building works. The position of the existing mains drains and any other mains services, including gas and electricity, and where they enter and leave the site, must be given every consideration.

This does not necessarily mean that any huge additional expense will be incurred because that will depend upon the depth of the pipes and services, but if drainage alterations are required, then these must be included in the plans. Amendments or alterations to mains services other than the drainage system must be discussed with the service provider before firm plans are made. Significant cost may be involved if a complete relocation of services is required, so it will be wise to check before any work commences.

Building on a sloping site.

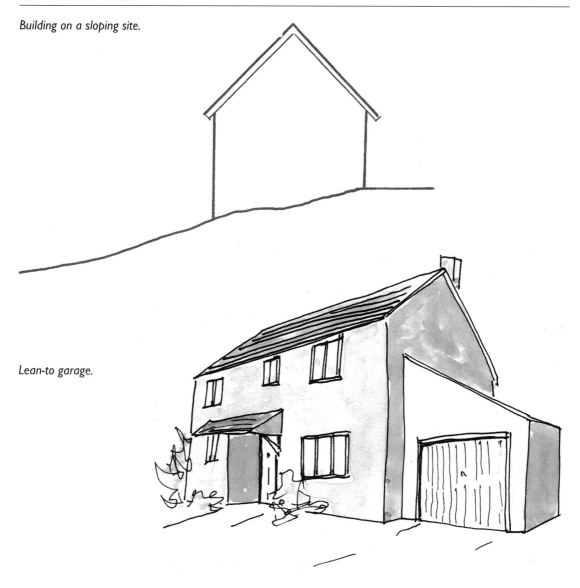

Lean-to garage.

Professional Advice

Where this process becomes just too complicated and it looks as if a number of problems will thwart the original plan, then the best solution will be to call in a professional. Contact the architect or draughtsman whom you would like to prepare the final plans, and arrange a meeting, on site, where your requirements can be discussed in full.

PLANNING AHEAD

When the location, size and extent of the proposed work has been decided, then the next consideration is whether or not this new work requires the approval of the local authority. There are often clear parameters within which the developer must remain, and boundaries around the property that must be respected. If there is any uncertainty about what is and is not permissible, then the best place to start is the local planning

*Garages built in front of
the building line.*

office. So before you go to the expense of professional building plans, take a sketch of your proposals showing clearly all the existing and immediately neighbouring properties, and discuss your plans with your designated officer. You may find that planning permission is not required, and that the work falls within permissible development, in which case only building regulations requirements need to be met.

On the other hand there may be any number of reasons why planning approval is required.

These will include the amount of existing development already on the site, other extensions, the building may be the subject of a listed building or preservation order, and the position of the building line may need to be taken into consideration. Whatever the reason, full plans will need to be submitted, either to the planning officer or to a full planning committee.

A clue to any requirements may actually lie within the area you live. With the vast majority of houses and bungalows built in estate locations,

Attached garage and store.

Integral garage.

the likelihood of someone within the area carrying out a similar project will be extremely high. If you do live in such a location, take the opportunity to wander round and see what others have done. And if you find a construction similar to the one you are planning, call in and ask the owner if they would mind showing you the completed work. Ask them to explain the benefits and the pitfalls, and glean from them the reaction they received from the local authority. It is likely they will extol the virtues of their new addition, wondering how on earth they managed without it, but listen for the 'buts' as well. Perhaps the access would work better elsewhere. Perhaps the layout should have been larger. Try to gain from the experience of others.

During this decisions-making process it is also important that you do not lose sight of what effect, if any, the new building work will have on your neighbours. It may be that the development in itself will not be a problem, but the amount of work that is involved, the noise, the mess and the regular delivery of building materials could put a strain on even the closest relationship. Therefore, try to involve your neighbours from the very beginning. Show them your plans and try to prepare them for the potential inconvenience to come. It will be important, at this point, to remember that where planning permission is required the local authority will consult the neighbours for their appraisal of the proposed works, so early approval will be an excellent starting point.

Opening the up-and-over garage door.

CHAPTER 3

Making Plans

The addition of a new garage could improve a property from both a practical and a financial perspective; this might be a barn conversion, or the restructuring of an outbuilding so it can be used as a garage. Such a project can be quite simple, or it can be more characterful in design, and incorporated within the parameters of the existing property, or accommodated within an existing layout and design.

Inevitably, building a new garage will alter the elevations and layout of the existing building. The inclusion of new garage doors, windows and external doors, along with a new driveway and possibly a new access, will alter the dynamics substantially and affect the area of garden. And it may be that all this will not have the right effect on either the property itself or the surrounding buildings: it is quite conceivable that such a dramatic change could produce quite the wrong result.

New garage with shingle driveway.

Where this is the case and the existing appearance is adversely affected once the garage door and driveway are in place, then possibly other ways to include the new structure may need to be considered.

THE DETACHED GARAGE

Where the proposed garage is to be completely detached from the main property, discussions with the planning officer will determine what would and would not be accepted. There is a huge range of possibilities as far as size and design are concerned, and of course the owner's personal requirements may be for more than just off-road vehicle storage. Furthermore, a detached garage can be classed as an individual property, so the size and layout may be subject to some scrutiny by the planning officer where a change of use to a dwelling could possibly arise in the future.

Another factor will be the materials to be used in construction, as they will need to be compatible with the existing buildings on the site and the surrounding area. However, this type of development may be obstructed by the planning officers, and the further away from the main building it is, the more likely they will look closely at the plans and will treat the proposals as a new building would be treated. The proximity to the main building will be vital, and there may well be restrictions on how much development is allowed. Planning officers are often well aware how precedents can be set, so look around the area to see if anyone else has carried out a similar construction that can be used as a guide.

In view of the huge variety of possibilities available when considering a new garage development, both single storey and two storey, it is difficult to provide a general rule on which decisions would ultimately be based. However, you can be confident in the fact that each project will be judged on its own individual merits, and on the effect the work will finally have on both the existing building and the buildings within the immediate area.

Sectional garage with up-and-over door.

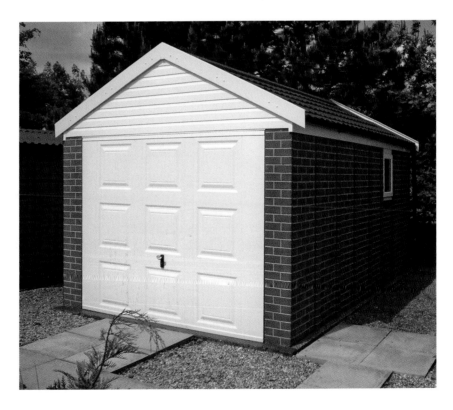

THE ATTACHED GARAGE

An attached garage is where the new work attaches to the existing dwelling or dwellings. Lack of space is often the reason a garage is attached to the existing dwelling, and where this is the case the boundary locations and considerations may well play a very important part in any proposed new development work. This design is very common on modern estate-built homes, where an attached garage does not require large amounts of land for it to work successfully.

The problems inherent with building on or against the boundary line should, of course, be discussed with your neighbour to avoid future dissension, and plans showing how the party wall or any dividing structure separates the properties are best agreed before any further building plans are drawn up. Building above an attached garage may also be a possibility even where it is not planned at this stage, so this is a point that should be considered before final plans are prepared.

As with any new development, conversion or extension work, whether you need planning permission or not will depend on both the individual merits of the work involved, and how the local authority views the work when compared with the local development plan.

THE INTEGRAL GARAGE

In many inner city areas, pre-war and even post-war developments were of attached or terraced houses designed in rows, at a time when garaging a vehicle would not even have been considered. More recently, and with building land in such short supply, the larger developers have often utilized every inch of space, thereby greatly reducing the possibility of further enlargement or extension: to achieve the maximum number of dwellings on a building plot, designers will exploit every opportunity to save space. A garage per dwelling would therefore have been very low on the list of priorities, and as a result on-street parking became

Two-bay garage with room over.

Detached garage with office.

popular. This has continued until the point has now been reached where the number of vehicles has clearly outstripped the number of parking slots available.

One increasingly popular method of reclaiming an off-street parking space has been altering a property to include an integral garage, located within the main structure of the existing building. In this way the 'footprint' of the building remains constant and the amount of land it occupies is not affected: the developer can work within the building structure without altering its size or the amount of land required. For conversion purposes where the garage is going to be integral to the building this will represent possibly the most complicated of conversion projects. Unfortunately the amount of room available is likely to be limited to the size of the existing dwelling; additions and extensions that extend beyond the building line will almost certainly require very detailed plans, and planning permission may be required.

REQUIREMENTS FOR PLANNING PERMISSION

Building a new garage or upgrading an existing outbuilding may or may not involve the same requirements as when building a new home extension, in that there is already a dwelling on the site; however, the project may still need the approval of the local authority planning department. Any existing building to be upgraded may be only a temporary structure, and may not have been included on the plans when the original planning approval was given. If this is the case, then planning permission may be required, and if the building is listed, then plans to build should be discussed with the local planning officer before anything firm is decided: where the building is listed, the amount of work that can be done without affecting its protected status could be limited.

For these and many other reasons it is important to find out as early as possible whether your proposals are, or are not, in line with local

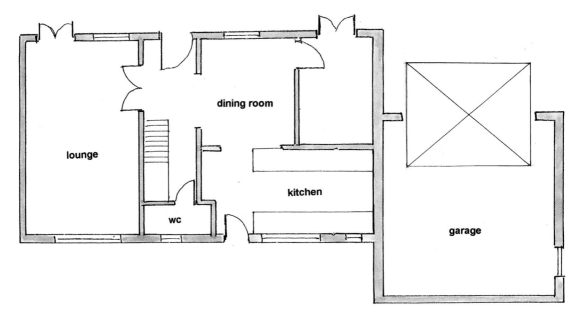

Layout showing attached double garage.

development plans. The local development plan will be available at your planning department, and will outline all aspects of the planning and environmental policies that the council has adopted, and how they intend to carry them out. It is important at this stage to remember that the local authority planning department provides an invaluable service to the local community. In particular it is charged with preventing excessive over-development, or what is commonly known as 'urban sprawl', while protecting 'Green Belt' areas and retaining the balance and character of the area as a whole.

Many new building projects will not require planning permission. Under local permitted development rules, garages, conversions and some smaller home extensions of a certain volume and in specific positions require only building regulations approval. However, this also means that it is possible to build an unsympathetic and poorly designed conversion that can seriously affect the value of your property, create problems with your neighbours, and alter the general appearance of the area as a whole. Sadly these occurrences are not unusual, and underline the need to discuss

proposals with the local planning officer before firm plans are made.

Where a planning application is required, the planning department will provide the necessary forms and will tell you how many need to be completed, the plans required and the appropriate fees. If the new building work is likely to be either extensive or controversial, then it may be wise to recruit the services of a professional. The quality of the application and the details shown on the plans may swing things in your favour if the decision is close. On the other hand, when the likelihood of approval is slim you can keep costs down by perhaps providing just sketch outlines in order to 'test the water'.

When it is clear that the proposals will meet with the satisfaction of the planning officer or the planning committee, then detailed drawings will be required to show the full extent of the new work. This should include front, rear and side elevations showing what effect the new work will have on the existing building, plus an overhead view, a block plan showing the immediate area around the building, and an area plan showing the effect on properties in the immediate vicinity. Planning permission

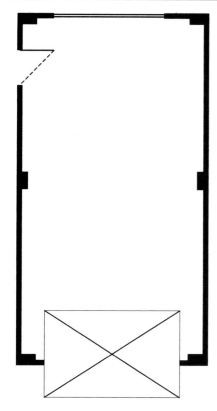

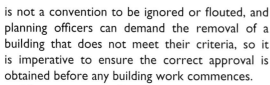

Single garage layout

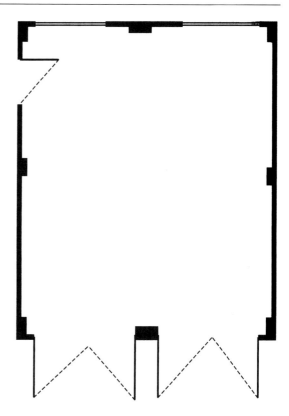

Double garage layout

is not a convention to be ignored or flouted, and planning officers can demand the removal of a building that does not meet their criteria, so it is imperative to ensure the correct approval is obtained before any building work commences.

Of course, not all development works will require planning permission, and there is also a scheme in place called the 'Permitted Development Scheme', which takes into consideration the extent of building already completed on the site. However, where this 'permitted' figure is exceeded, or if the new work is likely to exceed it, then planning permission will automatically be required. Again, further discussion with the planning officer will help to determine any action that should be taken.

Listed Building Consent

Where the existing building is listed, proposals to build a new garage must be discussed in detail; it

is unlikely that anything unsympathetic, including new builds, alterations and additions, will be permitted where the building is officially 'listed'. Such a project may also require listed building consent as well as planning permission: this is a separate application and approval demanded by the council, and it is likely that more detailed drawings will be required, showing the present building and the proposed additions.

Building Regulations

Whether your new development does or does not require planning permission, it will need building regulations approval. Building regulations are rules approved by parliament, laid down to ensure that minimum design and construction standards are achieved in domestic and commercial buildings. The regulations are a list of requirements, referred to as Schedule 1, and designed to ensure the health and safety of people in and around the building, including adequate access to, and facilities for the disabled and the elderly, and, very importantly, provisions for energy conservation.

Also included in the list of works requiring building regulations approval are alterations and additions to the drainage system, and additions to washing and sanitary facilities; and construction work that alters the use of a building or is likely to have implications on adjacent properties – for example, work on party walls and underpinning.

To make an application for building regulations approval there are three possible options to be considered: standard, speedier and specialized application.

Standard Application
The first and indeed the most common application for new build, conversion and extension work is a full plans application: this incorporates detailed plans, clearly showing all the proposed building works and all associated constructional details. When the plans are completed they will be submitted to the local authority building control department for inspection. When the plans are submitted the building inspector will check them to ensure the design of the proposed structure meets all the requirements of the building regulations. If not, then the plans will fail, and the areas in question will be listed so they can be redesigned or upgraded. When the plans are approved an approval notice will be given – approval of the plans, that is – then the work will be inspected in progress to ensure that it meets with the terms agreed on the plans.

Speedier Application
The second type of application is a building notice. Application plans are not required, though all sections of the work will need to be inspected by the building inspector as it progresses. This will greatly reduce waiting time for plans to be approved, but the work must comply in all respects with building regulations. This type of application can be used where time is short and where the contractor is fully up to speed with building regulations requirements, or it may be more suitable for small conversions and minor alterations than any of the range of more extensive improvements.

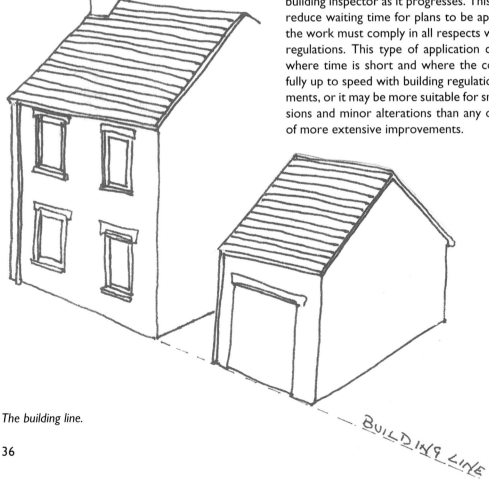

The building line.

Concrete reinforcement mesh.

Specialized Application

A third possible option is using an approved inspector, who will check the building plans and oversee the building work; when the work is completed to his satisfaction, an approval certificate will be issued. If the work is not completed to his satisfaction – and it is important to remember that this applies to all other applications as well – an approval will not be issued. When this happens the inspector will be obliged to inform the local authority so they can then consider the powers of enforcement available to them.

Bridge over pipes using concrete-reinforced lintels.

Fee Structures

Whichever application you choose, a fee or fees is required. A scale showing the amount to be paid, applicable to the size and value of the project, is available at the planning office. A full plans application involves two payments: a plan fee when the plans are submitted and an inspection fee due after the first inspection. Under a building notice only one fee is payable, and is the equivalent of the full plans application, payable at the time the notice is given. Full details of the fee structures, all subject to VAT, can be obtained from your local authority building control department.

If you choose to employ an approved inspector, then the fee to be paid is a matter of arrangement between you and the inspector. This fee is also subject to VAT.

For the majority of new-build garages, detailed plans will be extremely helpful during the construction process and will prove invaluable, initially, when obtaining quotations from builders and subcontractors. For these reasons a 'full plans' application is recommended.

The Structural Survey

The extent of the work required to build, improve, upgrade and convert existing buildings may not be immediately obvious, and will only become clear after a thorough survey of the property is carried out. Armed with an outline of the proposed building work, the surveyor will calculate the suitability of the existing site and surrounding area, and also determine what is required to achieve building regulations standards. The depth of existing foundations, the strength of the walls, the floor and the roof, will all fall within the requirements of a survey.

Recruiting a surveyor will not be required in all instances: where the building work is straightforward, a competent DIY-er may well be able to

Will mains water be required in the garage?

BUILDING LINE —

Above: Building in front of the building line will require planning permission.

Below: Brick pier adding strength to a single-skin brick wall.

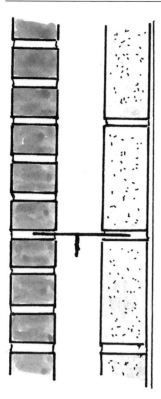

Cavity construction with wall tie fitted.

HIRING A PROFESSIONAL

To maximize the potential of your property and to capitalize on the experience of qualified professionals, especially where personal experience is limited, it is wise to use an architect or draughtsman to prepare your building plans. It is possible to draw them yourself, but the specific structural

work with the building control officer to ensure the structure is built off secure foundations and is structurally sound. The majority of attached garages are built initially with single brick walls and not the cavity walls required for living accommodation. For this reason, in some cases the foundations required will need to meet building regulations approval, and the open trenches will be inspected by the building control officer before concrete foundations can be laid. Where there is doubt about the site or the effect the new build will have on existing building structures, the building control officer may request professional approval in the form of structural calculations. These can be obtained from the architect or from a structural engineer.

For best results always use experienced tradesmen.

details required for building regulations alone can be daunting. By using a professional you can be confident that the additional expertise available will work in your favour.

The choice between an architect and a draughtsman is not so clear and is often made on cost alone, with architect's fees generally higher than those of a draughtsman. A qualified architect will have had extensive training and design experience and can be used to better advantage where these design skills are required. For small home extensions the draughtsman may prove to be the ideal and cost-effective solution, whereas extensions and alterations to older or listed properties may benefit hugely from the design expertise of the architect.

Fees will be calculated according to the work involved, so an accurate quote must be obtained before you give the go-ahead for plans to be prepared. Check what the fee includes, and who will pay the local authority application fees, and ask if any provision has been made should structural calculations be required. An outline of the possible fee may be given over the telephone, followed by a firm quotation after a site visit.

Step by Step

- Before deciding to build a new garage, make sure the space used for the building, the driveway and the access to the site are not overtly detrimental to the property as a whole.
- Look carefully at what the effect of the new build will have on the existing property and neighbouring properties.
- Carry out a limited survey to consider the possible extent of the work required, and what limitations there may be.
- Check with the local authority planning department as to whether planning permission is required.
- Where extensive structural work is planned, arrange for a survey of the existing property to be carried out by the architect or draughtsman, to determine what, if any, upgrading is required.
- Where the garage is expected to be situated close to or along the boundary line, discuss plans with your neighbour to allay fears and encourage approval.
- Of course your plans may not be original. It is always a good idea to check in the local area to see if similar work has been carried out, and what effect it has had on both the property and its function.

CHAPTER 4

Internal Preparations

When planning permission and building regulations requirements have been dealt with, then the next step will almost inevitably be to organize an architect or draughtsman to prepare detailed drawings for submission to the local authority for approval. It is possible, even with very little experience, to draw up building plans of a standard good enough to be accepted by the council, but often the structural requirements of a building regulations application can prove daunting. For this reason it is advisable to recruit an architect or draughtsman to prepare the building plans: this will maximize the potential of the property since it capitalizes on the experience of a qualified professional – using professionals at this stage can add a certain authority to the application that may well work in your favour.

Whether to choose an architect or a draughtsman may not be at all clear, so the decision can often be based on finances alone. Choosing for monetary reasons at this stage is not necessarily a bad thing, and where the property is modern and the work straightforward, paying extra for the services of an architect may not be money well spent. On the other hand, for older and 'listed' properties, and where the structure is heavy on design and new ideas, then the experience and guidance of an architect will be money well spent.

Architectural fees will be calculated according to the work involved, so an accurate quotation of the fee should be obtained before you give the go-ahead for plans to be prepared. If changes are made to the original plans then there are likely to be extra costs involved. Always check at each stage what is, and what is not included in the fee. There will also be a fee payable to the local authority. Cheques should be made out to the local authority, not the architect, when the plans are submitted; there may be additional costs if structural calculations are required. An outline of the cost involved may be given on first contact, over the telephone, then determined after a site visit.

When the plans are completed and submitted to the local authority for approval, then quotations can be obtained from contractors for all or part of the work. At this stage it is important to remember that the plans may not be approved as they stand, and changes may need to be made. This can cause confusion when the contractor quotes for one thing and is then expected to build something quite different; for this reason it is often best to wait until the plans are passed before approaching tradesmen and contractors for quotes.

PREPARING A FLOW CHART

It is at this stage of the project that its size and the time frame involved in carrying it out become more important. When local authority approval is given for a project there is normally a time limit within which work is expected to start; when planning permission is granted but the work is not started within the stated time, a fresh application may be required. Other important factors to be considered include obtaining quotations from tradesmen, arranging deliveries of materials and setting out storage areas. For this reason keeping

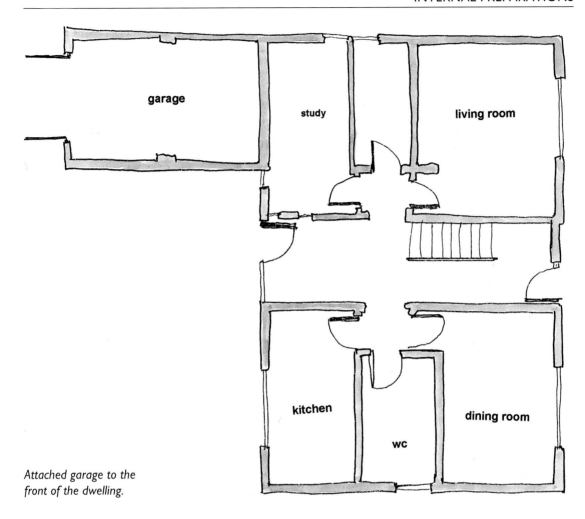

Attached garage to the front of the dwelling.

an accurate diary or flow chart showing each stage of the work, the date of deliveries, and the arrival and completion of the different trades is important.

The accuracy of the flow chart will depend upon good planning, and the art of good planning is confidence. If you feel confident that this whole project is merely an opportunity to progress and succeed, rather than a problem to be solved, then the whole experience will be both beneficial and rewarding.

How this record of future events is kept will be left to the individual. Some prefer a computer spreadsheet showing predicted times, dates and deliveries, accompanied by another spreadsheet showing what actually happened; others keep a diary; and yet others use a flow chart designed just for one particular project. Whatever is used, it must be kept up to date and the information included must be accurate.

Before any or all of this information can be collated effectively, quotations from suppliers and tradesmen will be required. This need not be a 'chicken and egg' situation, as it is likely that the materials required will be readily available, often within a day or two, whereas the tradesmen could well be booked up some months in advance. So unless the materials required are unusual and non standard, such as matching bricks and roof slates, or hand-made windows, it will be best to approach the trades first so they can be added to the time-frame before material deliveries are requested.

ADDITIONAL PLANS

The flow chart you prepare will show how the building work is expected to progress. It will simply be a diary of planned events showing how and when materials arrive, and what date tradesmen are expected to start and finish their particular section of the work. To accompany the flow chart there will inevitably need to be other plans, around which the success of the project will also be determined, plans not prepared by the architect but necessary for the tradesmen to work from.

The most important set of plans will be those prepared by the architect and from which the new structure will be built. These plans will include any new drainage, because drainage is subject to building regulations, but they may not include the other services such as gas, electricity and central heating. Where these are absent an additional sketch plan should be prepared showing what is expected: for instance, additional radiators to be added to the existing system, and their location;

electrical power points and light fittings, how many and where.

All these will depend on what the new conversion is to be. It may be an annexe requiring kitchen facilities, or it may simply be an additional reception, or a dining room, where these services are not so important. Other plans, less important but necessary for the smooth running of the project, will include one showing any materials to be reused and those to be discarded; also a garden plan and a materials storage plan.

Contractors and tradesmen will need to see all these plans to ensure their work does not impinge on any of them. Undoing work can be expensive, and will throw the whole system into disarray.

OBTAINING QUOTATIONS: TRADESMEN

For the best possible results and to ensure the smooth running of your project, use the best tradesmen you can find. Quality may cost just a little more but its value is timeless and will repay you time and again in quiet satisfaction.

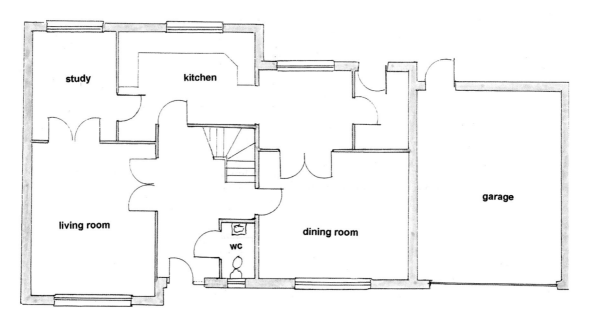

Attached garage to the side of the dwelling.

Always use suitable materials below ground level.

There is, however, no easy way to select the best tradesmen other than by word of mouth and reputation. Before making your selection, try to speak to at least a couple of previous customers, and if you feel it necessary, ask your building control department. It is unlikely they will go so far as to recommend an individual tradesman or company, but they may be able to help you with your selection and, importantly, steer you away from any unscrupulous operators.

After selecting the trades to quote for the project, make sure each has a clear view of the plans, and where possible visit the site. For smaller projects a site visit may not be necessary as there may be very little to see, but if, for example, the area to be converted is very confined and close to the boundary, then a site visit to see the extent of any problems would be wise.

The quotations should be given in writing to avoid any dispute, and should clearly outline all the work included in the price.

There are three clear categories for pricing work within the trade, and all are designed to ensure fair play to both parties. The first and most popular is a fixed price agreement where the tradesman agrees to complete a certain project for an agreed fee. This is an excellent method but relies upon both parties understanding clearly what is and is not included in the price. Where doubts arise, after a quotation is given, be sure to ask as many questions as necessary so that there are as few 'grey' areas as possible. All too often the home owner feels he has been 'ripped off' because the final bill bears no resemblance to the original quote. In the majority of cases this is based on a misunderstanding of exactly what was, or was not, included in the quote.

The second method is based on the amount of work involved, or a 'metreage' price. This method will be more applicable to plasterers and bricklayers where they work on a certain rate per metre of wall or per thousand bricks.

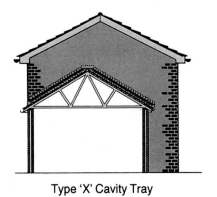

Type 'X' Cavity Tray

Where a garage abuts another building a cavity tray may be required.

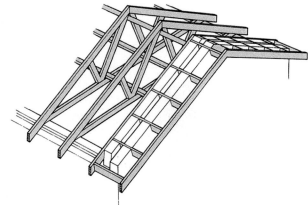

Gable Ladder

A typical gable ladder.

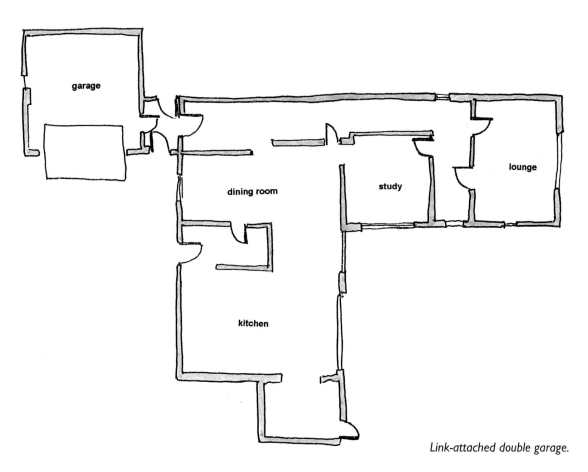

Link-attached double garage.

Clear the building site of all vegetative materials.

In many cases the full extent of the work involved may not be all that clear. Demolitions and excavations fall neatly into this category, and tradesmen or contractors may well hold back from giving a firm quotation for this type of work. Where this is the case the third, and in many cases more risky, method of 'day rate' is used. To say this method is 'risky' does not mean it is unfair or biased towards the contractor and away from the customer: on the contrary, this is a very fair way of getting work done to the satisfaction of both parties. There is, however, an element of risk in that close control of the work and a higher-than-usual level of honesty is often required to avoid large over-payments.

When the quotations are in, the selection process may be on price alone or on other factors. There is one line of thought that says you must accept the lowest price, but this is not always the case with smaller domestic projects where the emphasis is more likely to be on appearance and attitude, with the contract often going to the most suitable applicant.

With the quotation there must be time considerations. These will include when the tradesman can do the work, and should show how long the work will take to complete. Where the parameters of the project are clear and not subject to how other tradesmen keep to their particular schedule, then the time schedule should be easy to work with. On the other hand, chaos can reign where one tradesman holds up another and throws the best organized plans into disarray. For example, the plumber may not be able to complete additions to the central heating system because the plasterer has not completed his work. Very

47

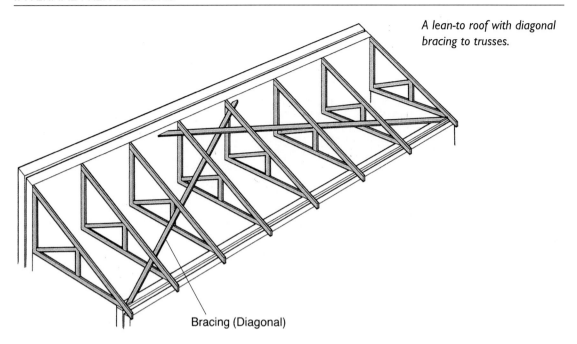

A lean-to roof with diagonal bracing to trusses.

Bracing (Diagonal)

small projects may easily be 'fitted in', but medium-length projects of a few days or a week may be more difficult.

Armed with the time schedules and availability, the spreadsheet or flow chart can be updated, and arrangements for deliveries of materials arranged.

OBTAINING QUOTATIONS: MATERIALS

After the plans have been approved and quotations obtained from tradesmen, then it will be time to organize materials. Depending upon the size of the project and the space available, materials will probably need to be ordered and delivered in phases. Where storage is limited, it is important to keep a closer eye on deliveries in order to avoid delays and disappointment should a tradesman arrive to start work only to find that all the materials necessary to complete his work are not available.

To get quotes for building materials, approach at least two local builders' merchants for prices. Where possible open a trade account and negotiate the best discount possible. If the project is substantial the builders' merchant may price for

supplying all the materials 'off plan'. To do this they will work from the approved drawings and quote for supplying all the materials. A good overall discount may be negotiated where this is the case.

Value Added Tax (VAT)

When calculating the total build costs, the inclusion of VAT cannot be avoided. This is an additional non-reclaimable cost to the project and can be significant. Materials suppliers will be required by law to charge VAT for the goods they supply, and this will be added, if not shown, to their invoices. The inclusion of VAT in prices at the outset may not be all that clear so it is important to ask whether or not VAT is included in the price you are given.

Paying VAT to builders, contractors and sub-contractors may be quite a different story. In the main, medium-sized builders – and this is determined on the building company's annual turnover – are required to charge VAT for their work, and to specify this clearly in their quotation. Where this is the case they must show, on the quotation, a current VAT reference number. This reference number must also be clearly shown on any invoice paid for work completed.

A lean-to roof with trusses secured with a binder.

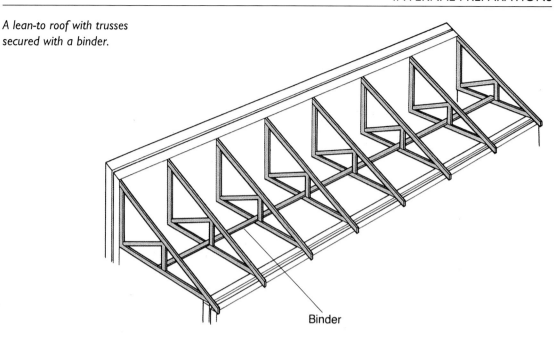

Binder

Unfortunately this taxation can be used and abused by the less scrupulous contractor, who may charge VAT when they are not registered and who see this as a way to make additional profit from the work. If you are not sure how authentic the contractor is, you can contact your local Customs and Excise office for advice. Adding VAT when it is not necessary can quickly increase the costs of a project without questions being asked.

Smaller builders and tradesmen are less likely to be VAT registered, so a note of caution here when a request for VAT is made. Again, check with the local Customs and Excise office if you are at all unsure.

FINDING A BUILDER

Smaller domestic building projects will generally be best served when a good local builder is employed to carry out the work. Of course, some money can be saved employing individual contractors to carry out their specific trades, but organizing this can reach nightmare proportions and is undoubtedly best left to the professionals. Finding a good local builder may not be as easy as it sounds, however,

and the media is constantly filled with stories to sharpen the mind.

When trying to find this 'golden nugget' in what may appear to be a sea of problems, there are certain guidelines to observe and rules to enforce. Finding a good builder will be the end of the story. Managing your builder to carry out the work within the agreed time and the agreed budget will involve some skill and a great deal of man management. Nevertheless, you will find that builders are, on the whole, a very honest and helpful bunch: they want to please, and they want to complete the project in the agreed time so they can then move on to the next project – and a good builder will always have a next project.

The first place to look for your established builder will be in the *Yellow Pages* – although the fact that a builder advertises in the *Yellow Pages* does not automatically mean he is a good builder. The reason for looking will be to identify the builders who are relatively local and whom you might consider. Draw up a shortlist. Builders specializing in smaller building projects will often be able to offer a more competitive price, and to recruit tradesmen used to working on smaller building projects. From this shortlist select three or four for further consideration. There is no hard and fast rule about this: if there were, life would be easy, but there is not. Some building companies will be newly formed and others may have been established for years, but neither signals a good or a less good builder. The following process is one that I feel will work in your favour and give you confidence in your selection.

First of all, contact all three builders. Tell them of your plans, and that you want to invite them to tender for your work. If they are happy with this, then ask if you can meet them, on site, on their current building project. This course of action may appear to be out of sequence, but it will give you a first class opportunity to see the 'ship they run', and should help you decide whether or not you would be happy with them carrying out your work. If you like what you see, invite each of them to visit you at home with a view to quoting for your work. If you contact a builder and he doesn't have a current project to visit, I suggest you either wait until he has one, or you select another builder. Make sure each builder quotes from the same set of drawings and for the same work.

When you have selected the builder of your choice you can seek references if you wish. Sadly this area concerning references can be flawed. I suggest you revisit the project you are already familiar with and speak to the owner. This way you can have a first hand, up-to-date knowledge of the builder's current work.

Lead flashings.

Understanding your Quotation

When the quotation arrives it should clearly state what is and is not included in the price. The building plans you provided will form a major part of this contract. If there are any grey areas, the quotation should clearly state this. If the builder feels that there is some part of the work he is unable to price accurately – underpinning the foundations, for example – it is quite acceptable for a provisional sum to be included in the quotation. If this section of the work is more difficult than anticipated, then there may be an additional cost after the provisional sum has run out. A provisional sum is not a ploy used by the builder to get more money: it is a safeguard to protect him and his business where certain aspects of the project may be just too difficult to price accurately.

For other items, the purchase of which will be decided at a later date – perhaps a bathroom suite, a new kitchen or a staircase – the builder may include a 'prime costs' sum. This is a fixed sum set aside for the purchase of that item. If the item exceeds that sum, then there will be the difference to pay; if it is less than the sum, then that will be taken off the final bill.

Provisional sums and prime costs sums are there to protect the builder and the customer. Leaving these to chance may result in the builder allowing for only a basic item, whereas the customer had in mind something a little more 'classy' or up-market.

METHODS OF PAYMENT

The old adage 'money talks' is as true in the construction industry as it is in any other walk of life. However, extra caution must be taken before handing over large sums of money. A building project may well be the largest single purchase made, excluding the mortgage, yet money is often freely handed out without fully considering the implications. Of course there are grey areas, and

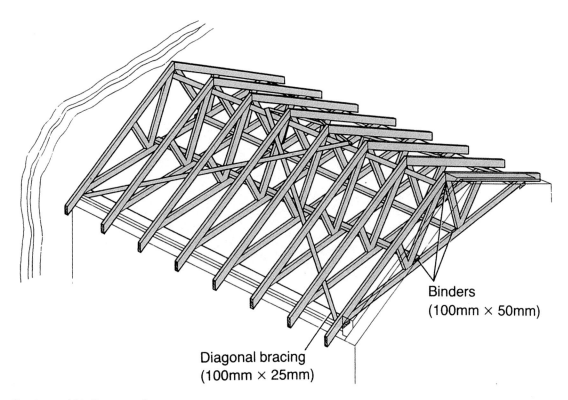

Binders
(100mm × 50mm)

Diagonal bracing
(100mm × 25mm)

Bracing and binding to roof trusses.

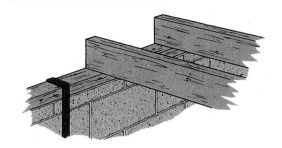

'Catnic' wall plate straps

TTL

TW

'Catnic' joist hangers

it isn't always easy to judge how much should be paid for each stage during a construction period, but these points must be clarified *before* any work commences. Do not pay in cash, and ask for an invoice every time payment is requested.

What is important – and it is my belief that more problems arise over money than any other area of work – is that clear and succinct methods of payment are agreed before deliveries are made and work commences. In general suppliers will want to be paid immediately, or within an agreed time period, before lorryloads of expensive materials are delivered. Some will expect payment before the delivery is made, others will accept cash on delivery (COD), and some will agree a monthly account. Whichever method you use, be sure only to pay for the materials supplied, and check every delivery to ensure you get exactly what you pay for. Do not accept shoddy or damaged goods, and return or replace anything you are not happy with.

Paying tradesmen will require more care, and making payments before any work is carried out must be avoided at all costs. In special circumstances a tradesman may ask for payment or a deposit towards expensive or special items: this is not unusual, nor is it unreasonable, though it should be specified in the quotation.

If you are asked to make a payment, or a deposit for any reason, proceed with a great deal of caution. There are two significant guides for making payments to tradesmen, and these support standard practice. The first and most common with private and domestic building works is when the tradesman expects to complete the work

within, for example, one week. It may then be agreed that a single payment will be paid on satisfactory completion of the work. When this is the agreement, then the money should be available, on time, as agreed.

The second method of payment, also common with private and domestic projects, is where the work will exceed one week and may run into several weeks. Of course it is unreasonable to expect the tradesman or men to work for long periods without payment, so a method of payment will need to be agreed, probably based on the work completed at the end of each stage. Knowing how much to pay is often difficult to assess, and must depend on how much work has been completed and how much is then left. Try not to overpay in the initial stages simply because work seems to be going a-pace, as this can leave little or no incentive for the contractors to complete the remaining work, especially where little or no money remains outstanding.

Hip roof detail.

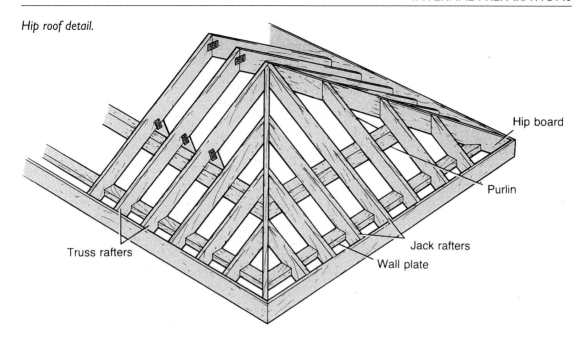

Hip board

Purlin

Jack rafters

Truss rafters

Wall plate

What is *not* standard practice, and should be strongly advised against, is payment for 'labour' before the work in question is completed or even started. Of course not all tradesmen – in fact, surprisingly few – are unscrupulous and overcharge, but being forewarned is being forearmed. It is well known that there is practically no area in life where we can avoid being duped, but I am confident that, if you follow these simple rules, pitfalls will be avoided. I am also confident that you will find the majority of skilled tradesmen put their reputation long before financial gain, and on completion of the project you will number several new names in your list of friends.

MANAGING MATERIALS

A significant part of the planning and success of any construction project, however large or small, will be the availability of both labour and materials: one cannot operate in isolation from the other. For this reason the art of managing incoming materials – and it *is* an art! – may well determine the overall smooth running of your project. Where room for storage is plentiful and there is also good, dry storage for the materials that

require protection from the weather, then deliveries can be received several days or even weeks before they are required. Some of the more delicate materials, which include cement powder and plaster, are considered to be best when they are fresh and will therefore benefit from being delivered just prior to use. Even where this is the case and storage is only very temporary, it will need to be suitable, ensuring the materials can be used when required.

Of course, the real art of managing materials can be seen when storage space is at a premium. A common sight is that of building materials piled high in and around front gardens, with heaps of sand and ballast often spilling over on to the pavement or highway. In these instances, and where good, dry storage is very limited, good planning is essential in order to eliminate problems, reduce waste, reduce the risk of theft and, very importantly, reduce the stress placed upon neighbours.

Where space is at a premium the deliveries will need to be well organized, and storage, even when very limited, must be adequate to prevent not only weather damage but also the likelihood of theft. The cost of materials stolen from

53

Templates may be required where frames are to be fitted after the walls are built.

building sites every year is staggering, with the often further unseen cost of delays to the building work itself.

When planning the overall storage package, try to ensure that all materials are quickly stored away, distributed around the site to where they will be required, and protected against bad weather when exposed to the elements.

SAFETY AND INSURANCE

On-site safety is of paramount importance, both for the occupants, for visitors and for contractors, with the emphasis on the developer to ensure that public liability insurance/site insurance is in place to protect all participants. Of course every possible precaution may be made as far as

54

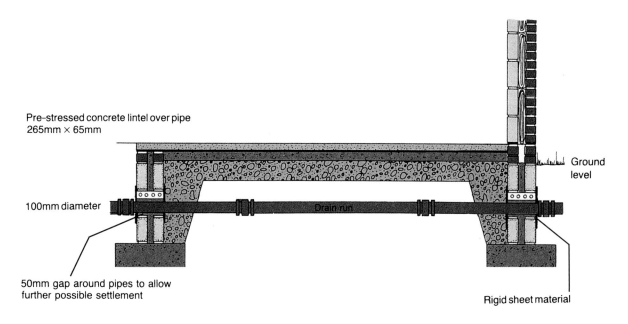

Pre-stressed concrete lintel over pipe
265mm × 65mm

Ground
level

100mm diameter

Drain run

50mm gap around pipes to allow
further possible settlement

Rigid sheet material

Building over existing pipes will require extra care.

on-site protection is concerned – scaffolding will be erected with handrails, and hard hats provided for visitors to the site – but there will be other members of the public for whom protective insurance is a must, including not only the house occupants, but visitors such as the postman and milkman. The tradesmen themselves are likely to have their own insurance and protective clothing, but unexpected and unusual circumstances do arise on site, and this insurance will at least provide the necessary personal and financial protection.

Risk Assessments

The requirement for risk assessments to be carried out before and during the construction process will depend on the number of workers working on site at any particular time. If you are the main contractor responsible for hiring in subcontract labour and for the overall site management, then the responsibility for carrying out risk assessments is yours. Where there is a main contractor, a builder for example, and it is their responsibility to both

hire in subcontract labour and deal with the overall running of the building site, then the responsibility for carrying out risk assessments is theirs.

Where the number of workers at any one time exceeds five, then at the time of writing a daily risk assessment is required, and diary notes should be made. It may be obvious to you that the area is hazardous, but do not take this for granted: barriers should be erected round holes and obstacles, and clear signs must be in full view. Other typical areas to assess include open trenches and scaffolding. Make sure that excavations are covered when they are not being worked on, that ladders are properly secured both top and bottom, and that scaffolding and scaffolding planks are not removed for use somewhere else on site or the structure tampered with. For example, a tradesman may temporarily require a plank to stand on, and removes one from the scaffolding but forgets to return it when the work is complete. This type of 'borrowing' will leave an area of high risk for anyone walking on the scaffolding.

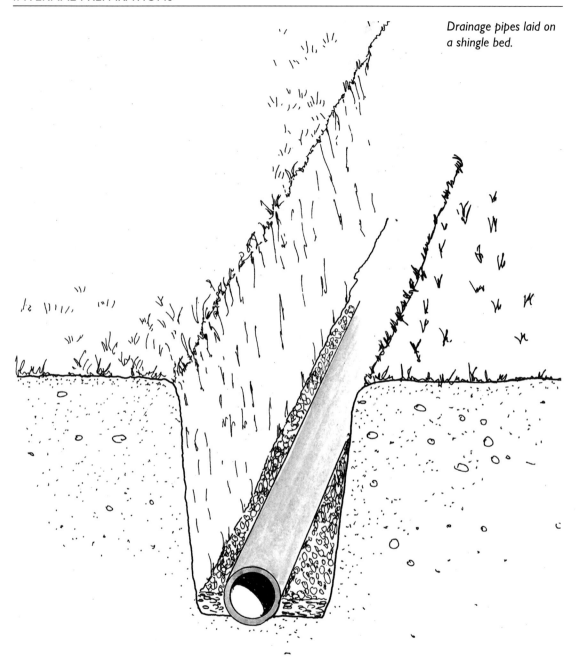

Drainage pipes laid on a shingle bed.

To make sure you do not fall foul of the insurance company's rules and regulations regarding site insurance, check with them about when you will be required to carry out risk assessments and what risk assessment notes they need. Any literature they can provide to help during the construction period will be very helpful. Of course builders, contractors and tradesmen will be required to have their own insurance, but they will still have the right to sue anyone responsible for the site should accidents occur due to the negligence of others.

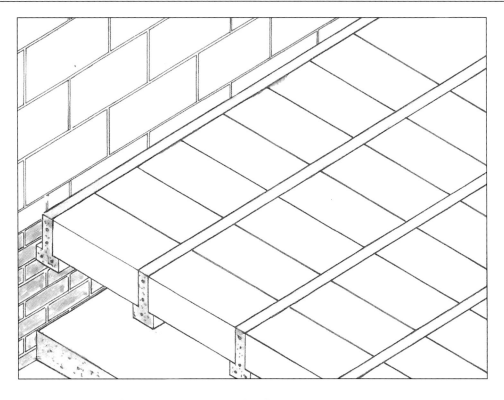

Where the proposed garage floor is suspect, a suspended floor may be acceptable.

Step by Step

- Select an architect or draughtsman to prepare the detailed drawings for application to the local authority for approval.
- When approval is received, discuss your plans with the skilled tradesmen and get quotations for the work.
- Break down the plans into material requirements, and get quotations from builders' merchants.
- Prepare a spreadsheet or flow chart showing material delivery times and the available dates of the key tradesmen.

- If you are using a local builder make sure you follow the appraisal procedure before getting quotes.
- Get quotations from at least three builders.
- Go through the complete project with them to ensure you both understand fully what is required.
- Make sure public liability/site insurance is in place.
- Carry out a risk assessment on the site every day workmen are there.

CHAPTER 5

External Preparations

With all the necessary paperwork in place, proper consideration can now be given to the practical elements of beginning this new project – and for this there is no 'one size fits all' rule. In fact to build a new building or to convert an existing one there will almost certainly be provisions linked to building regulations' approval. True, the plans prepared by the architect will comply, as they must, with building regulations, or they will not be approved.

On the ground, however, the detail may well be completely different. Take the foundations as a prime example: when the groundwork is being carried out for the garage to be built there is unlikely to have been an exact requirement in place to ensure that the foundations are excavated to a specified depth. In normal circumstances a foundation depth suitable for the building of a garage will be agreed on site with the building control officer, unless the garage is integral in

Store all materials safely.

Roof trusses will need to be ordered in advance.

design. The depth, width and indeed the specification of the concrete used for the foundation may be — in fact should be — clearly specified on the new building plans. This may be obvious from the outset, or further investigation may be required to establish the excavations needed.

Similarly with the garage floor there may well be variants depending on whether the garage is attached or detached. With a detached garage the floor will be installed for the purpose of being just a garage and is therefore likely to be set at a lower level than the existing house floor. The floor of an attached garage is likely to be compatible with the existing house floor levels. Investigations will be needed to ensure that full provision can be made to meet the new requirements.

In many restoration cases the complete removal of the existing building and a rebuild from scratch will be both the cheapest and the quickest option. Where an existing building or buildings are being removed or demolished and rebuilt to make way for the new building, then you will need to plan

for storage of the materials to be reused and for the disposal of all unwanted waste. Simple sketch plans along with instructions should be available during the discussion period with contractors so that everyone will be aware exactly what is to be salvaged, and where incoming materials are to be stored. Do not leave it to chance, as this can prove to be extremely costly and inconvenient. Recovering dumped materials, or relocating, say, a pile of sand to somewhere else on site can be time consuming and create unnecessary tension.

Whether you are building from scratch, removing and rebuilding, or simply filling in a gap between two existing buildings, full consideration will have to be given to any effect the work will have on your garden. Established trees and plants may need to be removed and relocated from where the new driveway is planned, or an existing driveway that runs into the garden area may also need redesigning. The storage of materials, the position of waste disposal bins, and even where cars will be parked during the construction work will have an impact on the garden. For this reason the new build, renovation or/and refurbishment cannot be treated in isolation.

MANAGEMENT OF ON-SITE MATERIALS AND EQUIPMENT

The very fact that this is a new garage can imply that space is at a premium, and this will be made even more restrictive because of parking space used for existing vehicles. It may be that all the weather-sensitive materials can be stored inside any existing buildings or temporary buildings as the building work continues. And it may also be clear that there is plenty of room for heaps of sand and stacks of bricks without affecting the general access to the home. Where this is the case and there is plenty of room, all too often the building works and heaps of materials spread out around the site in a way that would not happen if space were at a premium, so that eventually they occupy

All dry materials should be stored in a secure area.

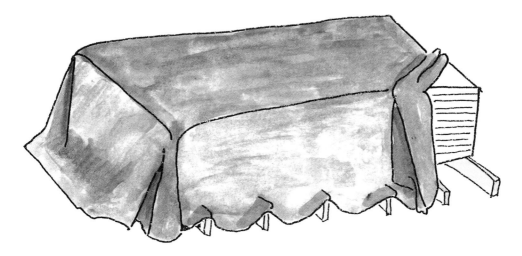

Timber and boards must be covered when not in use.

far more room than is necessary. On the other hand, where storage and access is at a premium, clever and skilful storage will reduce the impact on site and allow normal everyday life to proceed almost without a hitch.

Where materials are to be stored in the dry and there is enough space, then further protection may not be required: you only need concentrate on the proper rotation of the materials as they are used and as new deliveries arrive. Keeping a close eye on each stage of the building work will ensure that the materials for each particular stage are easily to hand, and not buried under materials to be used at a later stage of the construction.

Where the storage is outside, then naturally very much more care must be taken. These materials will include the bulkier items such as sand, bricks and blocks, and it is essential that these items are always covered as a protection against the weather by tarpaulins or similar. It is important to remember that hot, dry weather can be almost as damaging as wet weather, particularly with sand. The sheets can be removed as required, then replaced when not in use.

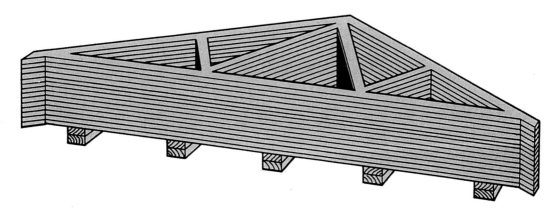

Stacking trusses.

Room to Work

Any new building will produce demands on space, and a new garage is no exception. By its very nature space will invariably be limited in the immediate proximity of the building, as well as around where it is to be built; if so, due consideration must be given to the room required for each trade to carry out the work involved. The balance between storage space and working space may be a very close call, but room for the tradesmen to carry out their trade is of primary importance, and the more space they have, the happier they will be. For this reason an area around and within the building to be constructed should be left completely free from hazards so that standard building practices can be pursued, such as the erection of scaffolding, and the transport of materials from their storage place to the point of use.

Plant and Equipment Hire

Plant and equipment hire is an absolute boon to the smaller building contractor, and invaluable to the do-it-yourself enthusiast, as it ensures that the larger items of plant and machinery required to carry out building projects quickly and professionally are both available and affordable. There are three clearly defined methods of plant hire associated with the building and construction industry: two are common to new build, home extension and loft conversion works, and the third can sometimes

Small plant can be hired by the day or week.

firms, and includes scaffolding and waste disposal skips. The third, and more common with larger development projects, includes items that are hired with an operative, such as JCB diggers with their driver, and tipper lorries with their driver. This method of hiring expensive plant and machinery to be used on minor works ensures the costs involved can be kept to a minimum, allowing all types of building project to fall well with the remit of the keen do-it-yourself enthusiast. Add to this the competitiveness of the now thriving plant hire business, and it is clear that this can only be good news for the end user.

There is a word of extreme caution, however. Many of the items available for hire can be very dangerous, even deadly, in the wrong hands or when used without the proper protective equipment. Make sure each item of equipment hired is done so *with* the correct protective clothing, goggles and attachments. The plant hirer should ensure these items are available at the point of hire, whether or not they are included in the price.

Hire or Buy?

Of course the contractor's equipment hire boon has been a revelation for the do-it-yourself industry as well, but there are times when hiring may be more costly than buying outright. Buying will inevitably involve larger up-front expenditure, but the project must be looked at in the round. Those tools that are just too expensive ever to be able to recoup the initial investment should be hired; however, other items that are less costly or used for longer periods may be another matter. In listing a few of the items of equipment required for new build, home extension and conversion works I have tried to be as cost effective as possible.

Equipment for Excavation Works

This section of the construction process will require small tools such as shovels and pickaxes, and may include a JCB, mini digger, skip and compactor. Of course it goes without saying that the purchase of a JCB for building a new garage may well be considered a slight overspend, and perhaps hiring major plant will always be the recommended

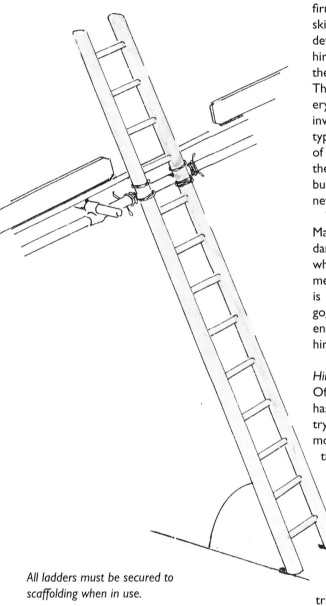

All ladders must be secured to scaffolding when in use.

be used with the larger building projects, and is more common to sizeable developments.

The first is the hire of items to be used by the hirer or the tradesmen employed by the hirer; these include cement mixers, tarpaulins, trestles, ladders and suchlike. The second is hired equipment delivered and erected by specialist

Portable toilets can be hired for small projects.

view. But smaller hand tools, as those mentioned above, and including shovels, a wheelbarrow, pickaxe, sledgehammer, crowbar, hosepipe and water butt, will almost certainly be better value to buy than to hire.

Tools for Wall and Roof Construction
This section of the construction will require a similarly wide variety of tools. Smaller tools will include spirit levels, trestles, ladders and a cement mixer; larger items might include scaffolding, planks, hoist and acrow props.

Due consideration must be given to each item in this category because trestles and acrow props do not readily fall into the DIY section of tools, and may never be used again. Try to calculate the length of time the items you are considering to hire will be required, and how the sums add up. Trestles will almost certainly get more use than, say, a set of acrow props, and that will go for planks as well.

There is also a buoyant second-hand sales market for many of or similar tools to the ones listed above, and you may well find that this avenue will provide many solutions to hiring or buying problems.

Tools apart, there is also a growing section of the hire market covering – and I use this word advisedly – such items as tarpaulins and dust sheets. Take a good look at everything you will require to complete the project in its entirety, and look at what tools the contractors will provide as part of their service; then list the rest, and look for the best solution.

Where the project is to be handed over to a builder in its entirety, the use of these items will have been included in their costings and no further payment should be required – unless of course unexpected items arise during the construction process necessitating a review of the price given. For example, the builder's initial quotation covering the depth of the foundations may have

Above: Larger plant can be hired by the day or week.

Below: Building over drainage pipes.

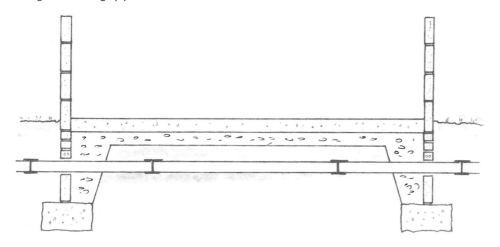

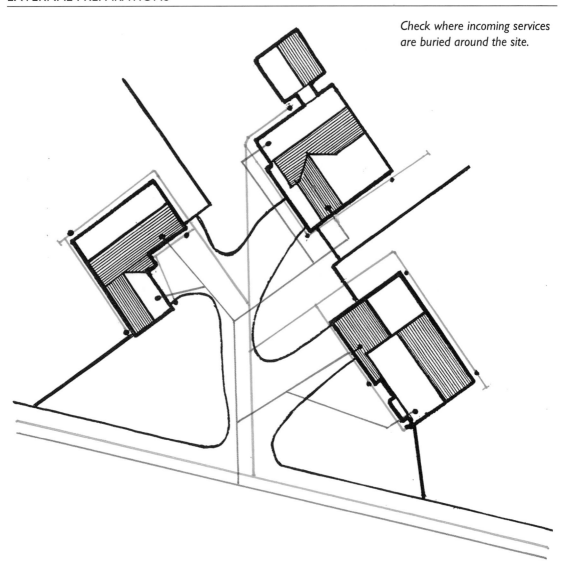

Check where incoming services are buried around the site.

specified a maximum depth of 1m, thus protecting his interests against unknown ground conditions. On site, however, the building inspector may demand foundations deeper than those specified by the builder, who may then have to bring in 'plant' or men to carry out this extra work, which will be an additional cost to the original quote.

Locating Existing Services
With new builds or where alteration works are substantial, especially when they are outside the existing perimeter of the building, it is important

to be aware of the location of incoming services. For those properties where gas, electricity and 'mains' drainage are connected, then it is very likely these services will all be situated close to the existing building. It is also likely that they will all access the site area from the road outside, either as a direct connection from the road area straight to the existing building, or buried around, close to and often in very close proximity to the existing building itself.

Needless to say, extra care must be taken where new excavations are carried out. Where

Clearly identify the area to be developed, and clear it of obstructions.

these services impinge on the excavation area they may need to be rerouted because building over them is not always the acceptable option. If the costs of relocation are high it may be advisable to seek professional advice before important decisions are made.

'Mains' drainage is a common building term for any waste water and sewage drainage connecting a property to either the main local drainage system or an individual system such as a sewage treatment plant or septic tank. The requirements of the building regulations will be the same, in that when rerouting 'mains' drainage, or when the plan is to build over existing drains, building regulations will apply so permission must be sought – if it is not already approved on the building plans – from the local authority building control.

PREPARING THE SITE

From an early stage the area where the work is to be carried out will have been designated in

principle. Where the new building work is within the existing building parameters (for an attached or integral garage) then the area concerned will need to be cleared of all obstacles, and the storage areas clearly defined. Where the work will extend outside the existing building parameters (as for a detached garage), then site clearance will become a priority before work can start.

These obstacles may simply be plants and moveable obstructions such as fencing or gates. More substantial obstacles requiring temporary removal may have been included in the contractor's agreement. Where the latter is the case, make sure the situation is fully understood with the contractor or tradesman who is expected to carry out this work. Delays and extra costs may well result where there is no clear agreement and work starts on the wrong footing.

This will also apply to the delivery of incoming materials. For bulky materials such as sand and bricks, clearly designated areas must be agreed and their location must be realistic. Delivery drivers will

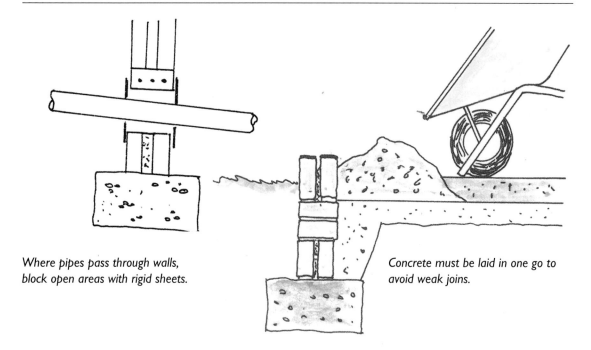

Where pipes pass through walls, block open areas with rigid sheets.

Concrete must be laid in one go to avoid weak joins.

be limited as to where they can comfortably access the site, and even with modern crane-operated vehicles, cannot be expected to search out storage areas suitable to tip their load. Where you, or your representative, cannot be on site to receive deliveries, always leave sensible instructions for the driver designating storage areas well within reach. When the materials delivered may be vulnerable to damage in bad weather and undercover storage is not possible, sheets or tarpaulins must be available to provide protection after off-loading.

Where excavation work is involved outside the line of the existing building, all visible obstructions such as paving slabs, plants and shrubs should be removed so that the precise area for this work can be marked out. Where obstructions are below the surface and their location is known, it may be wise to leave a clear indication of where they are so as to prevent the risk of an incident. The area to be excavated can be clearly marked with sand.

The majority of new detached garage buildings will be beyond the existing building line and behind it, so the spoil ensuing from the excavation works will need to be cleared so that the building work can be carried out successfully.

Waste Disposal
There is practically no area of the construction process where rubbish and waste materials will not be produced, often in abundance. A small proportion of the general building rubbish, or bricks, blocks or concrete from the existing buildings being removed or from demolitions, may be used as ballast to assist drainage in the soakaway. Some may also be suitable to backfill where foundation trenches have been produced, although it is always advisable to check with the local authority building inspector before old materials are buried in and around new builds.

It is advisable with any waste materials that you always check with the building inspector as to their suitability for purpose. For instance, some bricks will not be suitable for use below ground as they will degrade relatively quickly and will affect the building process.

Where excavations are carried out the topsoil can be dispersed around the site or sold off to neighbours. Waste and rubbish – and this will include subsoil from the trenches and oversite excavations – should be removed from the site at regular intervals so as to minimize mess. Working

Leaving a skip empty overnight may be tempting for local disposals.

in this way right from the start of work will keep the site tidy, and will encourage tradesmen and workers to do likewise.

The disposal of any building waste is proving to be a problem for local authorities. Fly tipping, typical of the lazy and unscrupulous, is not acceptable, and many areas now have clearly designated areas for waste disposal. If you don't know their location you should contact the council office.

There are two common methods of removing waste materials from site.

The first, and the popular choice for small domestic building projects, is the use of waste disposal skips. Skip hire companies are well known and plentiful in all areas, and this method of waste disposal is extremely popular, providing an excellent and competitive service. The skip or skips can be hired for an agreed period of time, and the hire charge will include any tipping charges, delivery to the site and collection.

One waste disposal skip can hold a large quantity of waste, and with good timing and regular contact with the skip supplier, it can be replaced, often at short notice, when it is full. Estimating how many skips will be required for the excavations may be tricky, but a calculated guess should

A skip provides excellent disposal of all building waste.

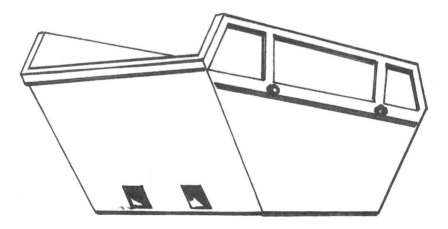

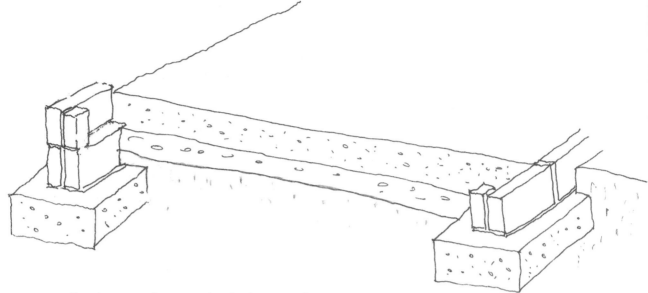

Foundations need not extend under the garage door area.

suffice. Soil increases in volume when dug, so calculate the volume of any excavation trenches, multiply the total by one and a half times, and this should give you an indication of the amount of soil that will be removed and how many skips you are likely to require.

When ordering a skip, try to arrange for its delivery early on the morning you expect to start work, leaving as much time as possible to fill it and get it removed, particularly if it has to be left in a place easily accessed by the general public. Leaving a skip empty overnight may well attract the attention of locals wanting to dispose of unwanted items such as old bicycles and discarded pieces of furniture, often under cover of darkness.

Before ordering a skip it is important to consider where it is to be left. Where the hire is short term, say a day or two, the position will not be so critical, but for a longer period, extra care should be taken. Also access points for leaving and removing the skip may be limited.

If the skip is to be left on the side of a public highway, the supplier must be given plenty of notice so that a licence can be obtained. If overnight hire is required, then lights must be arranged. The skip hire company will deal with these items

provided a suitable length of time is allowed. Do not leave a skip overnight on the public highway without lights; accidents do occur, and often result in prosecutions.

And finally, if it is not possible to fill the skip during the day, be sure to cover it overnight with a tarpaulin or similar.

The second, and often popular choice of waste disposal for smaller development projects is to hire a tipper lorry, with or without a driver. The waste soil and building rubbish can be disposed of at the local tipping site, for a fee, and the lorry can also be used for collecting small quantities of sand, ballast or pre-mix concrete. With smaller building projects, ordering small quantities of, say, sand and concrete can come at a premium when delivered to site, and these fees must be considered when making your calculations.

SAFETY ON SITE

Accidents do prevail on demolition and excavation works: every year many thousands of injuries and a number of deaths occur on building sites around the country, and many are preventable. To ensure your building site is safe, check regularly that open

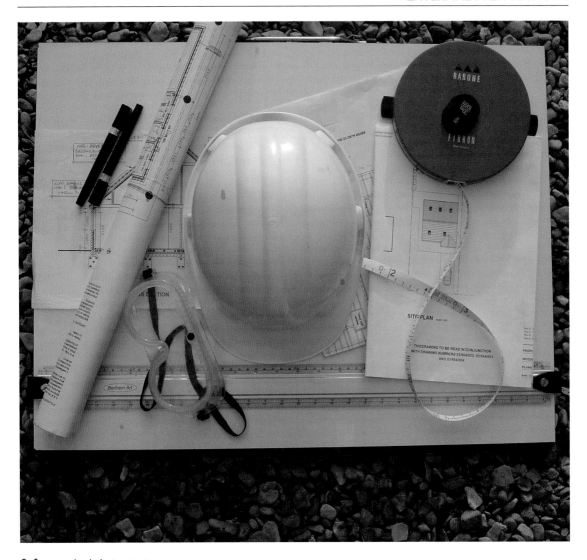

Safety on site is important.

trenches and excavations have barriers around them or/and are covered with planks or suchlike, to prevent accidents. Do not cover trenches and holes with sheeting or tarpaulins that simply hide the obstruction.

It is the responsibility of the main contractor to ensure that all equipment, whether owned or hired, is safeguarded against the potential to cause injury, and that all the necessary protective clothing – such as hard hats, gloves, goggles – is available on site should it be required.

Where any equipment is hired that may directly involve the use of protective clothing, then it is often the responsibility of the hire company to provide suitable protective clothing to be used with that particular piece of machinery, or to advise you that it is a requirement. However, do not leave anything to chance, and when hiring plant and machinery always ask the supplier about protective clothing. It is the responsibility of the subcontractor to ensure that proper shoes and clothing are worn to work for everyday site work.

Step by Step

- Check round the site where materials will be stored ready for use.
- Ensure work areas are not blocked off with materials or other obstructions.
- Check which items of machinery will be hired from plant hire specialists.
- Make sure that all contractors and tradesmen working on the site are familiar with the location of incoming services such as gas, water and electricity.
- Ensure that all garden plants to be relocated after the construction work is completed are set aside out of harm's way.
- Ensure that all contractors and tradesmen are familiar with all the materials that are to be saved from any demolitions and reused in the new building, and that they are stored in a safe place.
- Where waste disposal 'skips' are to be sited on the highway, make sure the hire company has plenty of notice so they can obtain the necessary licences. They will not leave a skip on the highway without a licence. Delays can arise.
- Where skips are located on a highway overnight, lights will be required to prevent accidents. The skip hire company will provide the necessary equipment.
- Site safety must be given the highest priority. Never leave holes and trenches open and unattended, and make sure that unsafe areas involving demolitions and building work are well guarded, and that notices to that effect are provided.

CHAPTER 6

Building the Foundations and the Damp Course

MARKING OUT THE TRENCHES

To comply with building regulations the site will need to be cleared of all obstructions and also all vegetative materials, plants and suchlike. This will also include the topsoil. The next thing to do is to mark out the trenches for excavation.

At this stage accuracy is very important if you are to ensure that the foundations are laid and the walls are built in the correct place. Check

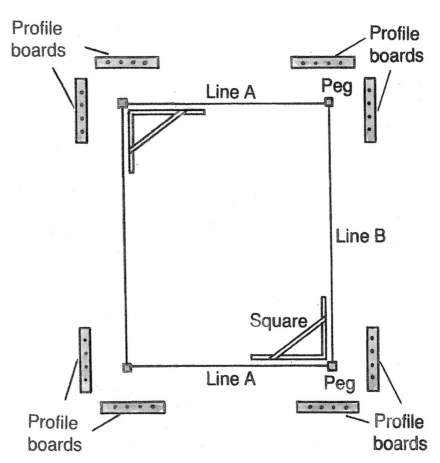

Setting up the profile boards before marking out the trenches.

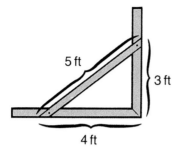

A builder's square.

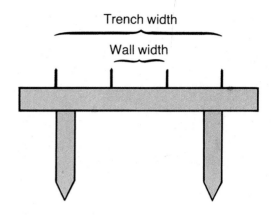

A profile board.

and double check the trench dimensions, and compare your calculations and positions with your approved building plans – and remember that it is only after the concrete foundations have been laid that positional changes required because of miscalculation become both difficult and expensive. You will find the positions and dimensions of the trenches clearly indicated on the approved plans. At an earlier stage you will have roughly marked out the whole area to be cleared for the new garage. Sand is often used to designate areas, but this next part of the construction will require a greater degree of accuracy. To set the foundation trenches out properly you will require a good spirit level, preferably 90cm (3ft) or longer, a length of good building line, at least four profile boards and a datum peg. The profile boards will be used as guides for foundations and walls, and the datum peg will be used to check levels.

The next step will be to select a level from which all future levels and measurements will be taken. As a rule, in the trade, the damp-proof course of existing buildings on the site will provide the best and most reliable guide to work from because it is static. The top of the datum peg should be set to reflect this level and transferred to the other parts of the new building. This level can then be used as a permanent guide from which all future levels are taken. A datum peg can easily be made from a length of wood, say 50 x 50mm (2 x 2in), then hammered into the ground at a good depth for stability; the top of the peg should be level with whichever existing guide you choose to use.

Position your datum at the furthest points from the existing building, but within a short distance

of the area to be excavated. If you place it too far away it will be difficult to work from, but if it is too close there will be a risk that it may be knocked over or moved. All datums should be checked regularly just in case of accidents to make sure that the new building level remains constant. You don't have to use the damp-proof course as a guide – you may prefer to use the existing floor level, as long as the guide you choose is on an existing building and is a fixed point.

As soon as the datum peg is in position, the profile boards can be erected. The top of each profile board must be level with the top of the datum peg. From these, and with the use of the builder's line, you can set out the foundation trenches and finished wall positions. The profile boards should be made from sturdy pieces of timber (see the picture [above]) and, like the datum pegs, must be checked regularly to make absolutely sure they are both level and square. For this, the most important part of the setting out, you will need a builder's square (see illustration *above*) to make sure that the corners are square and that the new walls abut the existing walls squarely as well.

If you can start at the existing house wall, then it is advisable to do so. Then, with the builder's square and a set of the building plans to guide you, attach the first string line to the existing house wall where the new garage wall is to begin, and at a point level with the datum peg, in this case the

*Marking the dpc level
with a datum peg.*

SETTING OUT

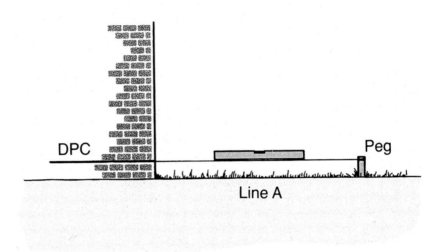

DPC   Peg

Line A

damp-proof course, level. Run the first string line (line 'A' on the illustration on page 73) away from the existing wall to a point at least 1.5m further than the garage measures. At this point the first profile board can be erected, using the builder's square to ensure it is parallel with the existing house wall, and a nail can be hammered into the profile board to attach the line. Repeat this process for the opposite wall.

The two string lines will now show two of the new garage wall positions. Measure along each line, indicating the garage width, and tie a small length of line as a guide. Using these ties as markers, the side

profile boards can be erected, again at about 1.5m from these string lines.

Next run a third length of builder's string line to intercept the two markers to nails on the side profiles: you now have the outer measurements of your new garage (line 'B'). Further nails and string lines can be added using measurements taken off the building plans. The two inner string lines show the internal and external position of the walls, and the outer string lines show the footings. When all the lines are in position, double check the measurements on site and on the building plans, and make sure all the corners are square using the

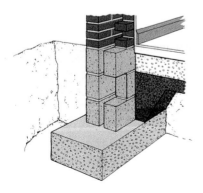

Strip foundations.

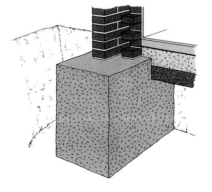

Trench fill foundations.

Pegs showing concrete depth.

builder's square. Next, remove the inner string lines and set them aside for later use; then mark the footing positions on the ground by trickling a clear line of sand directly over the outer string lines. When a clear outline is marked, these final string lines can be removed. You now have the footing positions marked ready for excavation.

The builder's string line can be replaced at any time if you want to check the positions. Only after the concrete foundations are laid and the bricklayer has built the garage walls up to damp-proof course level can the profile boards be removed. Always leave the datum peg in place until after the building works have been completed.

THE EXCAVATION WORKS

When all the preparations and setting out have been completed, the excavation works can begin. Only a few areas of construction work offer a choice of exactly how the work is carried out, and excavation is one of them. You can excavate by hand or by machine. Hand digging using shovels and a wheelbarrow can be extremely focusing and incredibly strenuous and is accompanied by a serious health warning: recovering in hospital from a body breakdown can play havoc with flow charts, so extreme caution is advised!

Digging footings by hand, or by any method, requires extreme caution. Careless excavations can cause damage to drainage pipes and incoming services: it is definitely not advisable to lacerate an electricity cable or a gas pipe with an over-energetic swing of a pickaxe. For larger construction works, or just to speed things up, you may decide to excavate the foundations using a mechanical digger, or JCB. But to do this – and I think it is reasonable to assume that the excavations will be carried out quickly – any time gained will be lost if soil disposal is not carried out with

Insert pegs to ensure a level foundation base is laid.

equal speed. For this reason, if you decide to use a mechanical digger, waste disposal skips are unlikely to be the best option, whereas a tipper lorry, hired with or without a driver, should prove ideal.

A tipper lorry – and they come in various sizes – can remove quite a large quantity of waste soil to the local tip in fairly quick time, enabling the excavation works to progress at a continuous rate. The tipper lorry is dual purpose in that, as well as removing waste materials from the site, it can also be used to bring materials such as sand and ballast to the site.

Another word of caution here: before you decide whether or not a mechanical digger is the best option, make sure there is plenty of room on the site for the work to be carried out successfully. In particular it is important that the digger, and the tipper lorry for that matter, has unobstructed access and plenty of room to manoeuvre in and out of the site.

Excavating Drainage Trenches

Any new drainage trenches can be excavated at the same time as the footings, retaining the soil for covering the pipes after they are laid and checked. The trenches should be only wide enough for the pipes, and deep enough, and at the required fall, for a 100mm layer of pea shingle on which the pipes will be laid. The trench depth will be determined by how deep the existing drainage pipes are, or according to the specifications on your plans.

Excavations for new inspection chambers (manholes) should also be made at the same time as the footing excavations; the concrete base for the inspection chambers can then be laid at the same time as the concrete foundations. At all times drainage excavations should be kept fairly tight, as excessive room is not necessary.

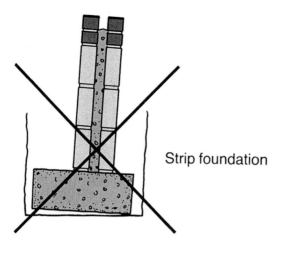

Strip foundation

Left: Always build walls off the centre of the foundation.

Below: Large machinery can be hired to carry out those heavy jobs.

Rainwater drainage can be discharged into a soakaway.

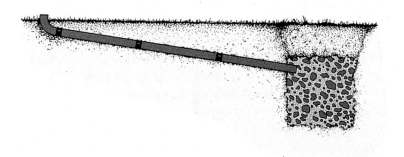

Excavating Soakaways

There are really only two options available to you for the disposal of surface water from hard surfaces and rainwater drainage from roofs. The first is through the existing surface water pipes and rainwater drainage system, and the second, and most common, is via a newly excavated soakaway.

The simple explanation of a soakaway, as shown on your plans, is just a large hole in the ground filled with rubble into which the rainwater and surface water will drain, and in the majority of cases that is exactly what happens. However, there is certainly more to it than that, in that the steering and collection of surface water into a soakaway

Foundation depths may differ depending upon the load imposed upon them.

Always stack materials safely on scaffolding.

will only work well if the permeability of the soil is good and allows it to. Digging trial pits and filling them with water to test this theory is one method; the other is to rely on local experience of soakaways, advice about which should be available from your local building control officer. Each soakaway should be positioned at least 5m from any other buildings, unless specified otherwise, and be at least Icu m in area. Digging the soakaway before the building work begins is to be recommended, as this will provide you with a hole in the ground into which broken blocks and bricks can be thrown as the building work progresses.

For obvious reasons of safety, try to make sure that the soakaway hole is covered with a rigid covering at all times. Once the soakaway is filled, it should be covered with an old sheet of perhaps corrugated tin or something of similar rigidity, and then covered over with at least 300mm of topsoil.

All pipes carrying rainwater to the soakaway from this, or any other new building, should be laid at a fall of at least 1 in 40, and must be suitable for the purpose.

Site Safety

Digging holes in the ground and excavating trenches provides the perfect opportunity for accidents to happen, so the greatest of care is required. Any holes or trenches left unattended *must* be covered, or at least roped off to prevent the unwary from stumbling into them. Greater care will be needed when weather or ground conditions fill the excavations with surface or ground water. Extensive barriers and warnings will not always prevent the unexpected when dangerous conditions prevail. Only leave holes and trenches unfilled for the shortest possible times.

BEGINNING THE BUILDING WORK

As soon as you have completed the excavation works the trenches must be inspected and approved by your building inspector. You will be asked to provide approximately twenty-four hours' notice to Building Control for the inspection to be carried out, and the trenches must be inspected before the concrete is poured. If the trench base is not completely secure and excavated to an acceptable standard to ensure the integrity and stability of the foundation concrete, you may well be asked to make whatever improvements are required, and this may include digging the footings a little deeper until the base is secure. Then, and only then, should you make plans for pouring in the concrete for the foundations.

At this time the builder's lines you removed from the profile boards to carry out the excavation work can be reinstated so that the depth of your trenches can be measured and the amount of concrete you require can be calculated. From this measurement wooden stakes can be driven into the base of the trench, at sensible intervals of about 2m apart, to provide a depth and level guide to work from when the foundation concrete is poured. To calculate the height at which each stake must be set, measure down from the reinstated builder's line, then drive the stake firmly into the trench base. Once the first stake is set at the required level, then, using a straight-edge and a spirit level, additional stakes can be driven into the trench base until the whole foundation area is set out.

Constructing a Gauge Rod

To help you set up the foundation depths and the wall heights from off the foundations, the best, and the most commonly used tool in the trade, is a gauge rod. The gauge rod can be constructed simply by using a piece of spare timber on to

Concrete foundations with a pier addition.

Secure concrete foundations.

Foundations good enough to build off.

The pier foundation laid as shown.

which you can plan the wall height at different levels, incorporating the materials to be used. It will be helpful to the bricklayers and the roofers, and you can calculate the foundation depth to coincide with brick or block measurements and finished wall measurements. For example, where the walls are built below ground level off the concrete footings and constructed using concrete blocks with a brickwork finish, where the wall is visible, the markings on your gauge rod will be made showing the number of blocks and bricks to be used plus the cement mortar bedding between each course.

Making a gauge rod before the concrete foundation is poured may help you avoid split courses of bricks or blocks because you can increase the foundation thickness accordingly. A split course of bricks may be used where the courses are calculated to be less than the height of a brick. This does happen occasionally, even with professionals, and is permissible below ground level and should not affect the overall integrity of the wall. By

setting the trench stakes to a depth acceptable to the measurements on the gauge rod, the courses of blocks and bricks should make up to complete courses.

Concrete Foundations

As far back as the 1920s concrete began to replace brick, and in some cases stone, as a foundation for walls and buildings. Previously hand mixed and now more commonly mixed in a concrete mixer, the foundations are there to bear and spread the load of the wall built off it. A typical concrete mix for foundations is known in the trade as a 1:3:6 mix, and consists of one part Portland cement (Portland cement is a complex, heat-treated mixture of lime, silicates and aluminium with iron oxides added) and nine parts ballast (already mixed at three parts sand and six parts gravel). When mixed with water the mixture undergoes a fairly rapid chemical reaction that transforms it into a hard, rock-like substance that has great strength.

Facing bricks can be used providing they are suitable for use below ground level.

Concrete blocks used below ground level.

Wider footings may be required for cavity wall construction.

New building foundations can be mixed on site or delivered, ready mixed, to be poured into the foundation trenches to a depth required by the building inspector. A specified foundation depth may be shown on your building plans, but this is flexible in that you can increase the thickness but not decrease it. There are two common types of concrete foundation, each having benefits of its own. The first and most popular is a strip foundation. Set in the bottom of the trench at a minimum agreed depth as specified on your building plans, the walls will be built centrally off the foundation to ensure stability.

The second type of foundation is a trench-fill foundation, which is, as it sounds, a concrete foundation filling the trench to within a short distance of the top. It is possible to build off the edge, and not centrally, of a trench-fill foundation, and is commonly used where walls are built as close to a boundary as is possible. The drawback with a trench-fill foundation is where drainage pipes pass through it: when this is the case the pipes should be well wrapped in a protective material padding, and positioned when the concrete is poured to avoid any damage as the foundations settle.

A raft foundation is the third and least common of foundations in use today. Raft foundations are more likely where landfill and subsidence is possible; often they consist of a reinforced slab up to 300mm below ground level, thickened up where the walls are to be built off the foundation. A polythene membrane will be laid on a sand-blinded hardcore base, then the first concrete layer of the raft is poured. A layer of reinforced mesh will be set in this layer, then another layer of concrete is poured. A second layer of mesh is set into this layer, then a final top layer of concrete is poured to finish.

The building area taking shape.

Footing showing the pier being built.

Pouring Concrete

Speed is the most important requirement when laying or pouring concrete. Mixing and then pouring the concrete should be a continuous process to ensure that each load bleeds in well with the previous load, thereby maintaining the overall strength of the concrete. Do not pour in a load, then leave it for an hour or so, then pour in the next load. Concrete soon becomes dry and unworkable, and by doing this a 'join' will be formed where the two loads meet and this join is a weak point in the foundation. When you are mixing the concrete by hand, at least one man should mix and pour while another levels off each load.

For larger jobs pre-mixed concrete from a ready-mix supplier will save a lot of work and speed up the process. The concrete will be delivered to a mix you specify – 1:3:6 is most usual for foundations, although ground conditions will dictate, and to a working consistency applicable to the circumstances. If the concrete can be poured directly into the footings all will be well, but where the concrete has to be dumped on to a large plastic sheet then wheelbarrowed to the trenches ask the supplier about adding a retarder. This will give you a little 'working' time, usually a couple of hours, before the concrete starts to dry out.

Ordering Concrete

When the concrete is ordered from a ready-mix supplier make sure you tell the supplier what the concrete is to be used for, the area you are covering and the depth you are filling to. Also let them know if you intend to dump the load on to a polythene sheet or if it is to be poured directly into the footings. Do not calculate how much concrete is required too exactly, and always allow a little extra for error. If, when the concrete is poured in, you have some left over, the lorry driver will usually take it away for you. If it has been dumped on a sheet and you have some left over and it cannot be used anywhere else on the site, spread it out as thinly as you can and leave it to dry. It can be then used as hardcore or ballast, on the oversite area for example. Do not leave it in a huge lump to be broken up later.

The cavity below ground level should be filled in with lean mix concrete.

Level off the oversite area ready for hardcore and concrete.

Trenches can be backfilled with hardcore and rubble.

Well compacted oversite area.

Walls Below Ground Level

When you have finished the footings and the concrete has had at least a couple of days to set – or 'cure', to be precise – the bricklayer can come in and build the walls up to damp-proof level. These walls will usually be built in blockwork and brickwork, or just brickwork, but make sure that the materials you use – blocks, bricks and cement – are suitable for walls below ground level. Not all materials are suitable for this purpose, and some will degenerate very quickly due to the extra moisture associated with being below ground.

After the foundations are laid you can use the gauge rod to calculate the number of blocks and bricks required to build the walls up to damp-proof course level.

Lintels

Where drainage pipes pass through or under the foundations, lintels will be required to act as a suitable bridge over the pipes. Below ground level, pre-stressed concrete lintels are the best option. As with all lintels, an end bearing – that is, the part of the lintel that rests on the walls adjacent to the opening in the wall – of 150mm must be allowed. This will leave openings around the pipe where burrowing animals can dig under the extension. To avoid this, cut a rigid sheet to fit round the pipe and to cover the hole in the wall, and secure it in place before backfilling the foundation trenches.

Underfloor Ventilation

Where the new garage abuts an existing property and that property has wooden floors, then ventilation must be provided to ensure a continuous and

A smooth surface ready for the damp-proof membrane to be laid.

free flow of air to the wooden floor area. This will help to prevent dry rot and other airborne fungi causing damage to existing and new wooden floors. This is likely to be more applicable to older properties where wooden floor joists and floorboards are common, and where the timbers are not or have not been treated against these perils. Airbricks will be available in the existing walls and you can use these openings for this ventilation to be maintained. Where the air under the floor becomes stale and stagnant, in corners for example, there is always a risk that air conditions will become suitable for such unwanted attacks. If you are installing a timber floor always use timbers treated against such fungal and insect attacks.

Precautions must also be taken when building against walls where existing airbricks are positioned to ensure that a free air flow is maintained. Where this occurs, new airbricks must be built into opposite external walls, and if the new building floor is concrete, the air can be ducted into the area at risk by way of pipes laid under the oversite concrete.

Airbricks

Where a solid concrete floor abuts an existing suspended wooden floor, adequate underflow ventilation must be provided from airbricks through ventilation pipes laid under the solid floor. Clay airbricks will be built into external walls at up to 3m apart and as far above ground level as possible, but below damp-proof level. In corners where stagnant air can become a problem the airbricks will be situated within 450mm of the corner.

A purpose-made clay ducting is available to continue the ventilation through the inner wall, and is built in with the airbrick.

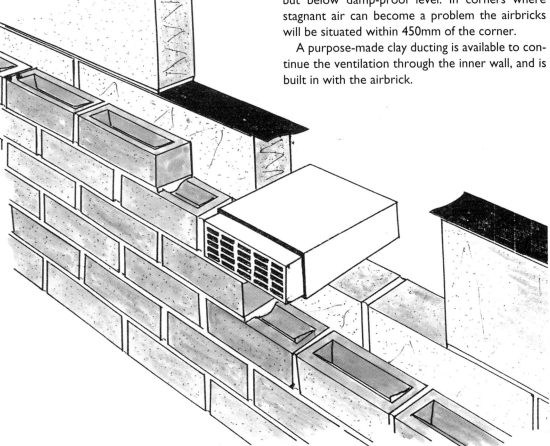

Where the newbuild abuts an existing building, airbricks may be required under the floor.

PREPARING THE OVERSITE

When the garage walls have been built up to damp-proof course level the area within the walls is called the 'oversite'. You may well have stripped all vegetation off this area at an earlier stage, but ensure that all topsoil, vegetative materials and perishables such as wood or roots are removed and that the area is cleared ready for the hardcore base to be laid. As a final precaution, and if you are in any doubt, spray the area with a good weedkiller before starting the next stage.

On this prepared oversite area lay a bed of clean hardcore evenly, and then compact it with a heavy compactor or a 'whacker plate' hired from your local plant hire centre. The hardcore should be laid to a depth of no less than 150mm and not greater than 300mm. Old broken bricks and roof tiles were often used to provide the best hardcore, but they are not always permitted, so follow instructions on the building plans and discuss possibilities with the building inspector. Make sure the hardcore base is of a material of manageable size to consolidate and compact without leaving unwanted air pockets.

If you are laying a damp-proof membrane on top of the hardcore and below the concrete oversite, the hardcore, when it is compacted, must be 'blinded' with at least 12mm of sharp sand to prevent the membrane being punctured by any sharp hardcore projections.

Concrete Floor Insulation

Depending upon what the building project comprises, you may or may not require concrete floor insulation. If the building is simply a garage, then it is unlikely, but if part is being used for domestic

Rigid insulation laid on to a damp-proof membrane.

The area should be smooth and clear of sharp objects.

purposes the insulation may be specified on the building plans. Building regulations specify that you must reduce any heat likely to be lost through the solid concrete floor, so to combat this, a layer of at least 25mm flooring-grade mineral fibre can be installed above the damp-proof membrane and below the concrete slab. This insulation layer can be laid on the membrane but below the concrete oversite, or on the concrete oversite but below the floor finish, concrete screed for example, if the concrete slab is not the finished floor.

There are other variations of concrete flooring insulation, and if your approved plans specify a variation, this should be followed.

Damp-Proof Course

To prevent dampness rising from ground level and causing damage to both internal and external

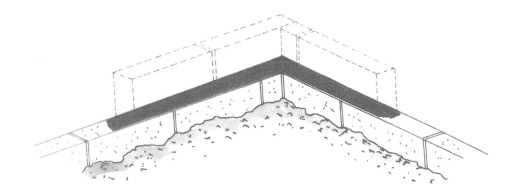

Horizontal damp-proof course approximately 150mm above ground level.

walls, a damp-proof course, or dpc, must be installed. The dpc will be fitted to all walls, and will be bedded on with mortar. Where the new dpc abuts any existing walls it will need to be dressed into the existing dpc to provide a continuous and preventative barrier. The dpc should be at least 150mm above ground level, and where this is not possible, when you are building into a bank or similar higher ground, all precautions must be taken to ensure that water penetration to the internal walls is prevented.

Damp-Proof Membrane

The damp-proof membrane will be installed to prevent damp rising through the concrete floor area. There are several methods in operation to prevent this, the most common being a membrane sheet laid on top of a sand-blinded bed before the concrete oversite is laid. Where the concrete oversite is not the finished floor, then liquid bitumen can be painted or laid hot on top of the concrete oversite and below the finished floor. With the first method a large polythene film membrane sheet, of a quality applicable for this purpose, must be laid on top of the sand-blinded base. When you do so you must make sure that all joins are watertight; also take the greatest care not to puncture the sheet before and during laying it on top of the oversite area, and take extra care again when pouring the concrete on to the sheet.

With the second method there are several proprietary brands of cold liquid bitumen solutions that can be painted on to the oversite concrete. Manufacturers' instructions must be followed carefully, and up to three coats will be required.

A well prepared oversite area.

A level and clean overside surface.

The third method is the use of hot bitumen, and this is often called 'tanking'. This is very applicable where an inspection pit is being built in the garage. The hot bitumen is painted on the vertical concrete and can be poured on to the primed oversite concrete area to a depth of not less than 3mm. Whichever method is chosen, it is important to remember that the floor membrane must be dressed up to and adjoin any existing and new damp-proof courses to provide an unbroken and continuous protection for the floor area.

Laying the Oversite Concrete

You have excavated the oversite area, laid and compacted the hardcore, and, if you are using a sheet damp-proof membrane, you have sand-blinded the hardcore and laid the membrane sheeting. Now the next step is to pour on the oversite concrete. Oversite concrete is commonly mixed at a 1:2:4 mix, which is slightly stronger than foundation concrete, which is commonly mixed at a ratio of 1:3:6. Laid to a minimum depth of 100mm, oversite concrete can be mixed on site or delivered ready mixed like the foundation concrete. If you are pouring the concrete on to a membrane, the greatest care must be taken not to puncture it, which may result in problems at a later date.

As the concrete is poured it must be levelled and tamped down to remove air pockets,

Base well compacted as required.

Concrete oversite laid showing damp-proof membrane.

Oversite concrete base.

then left to cure for up to three days. Unlike the foundation concrete where the concrete is unlikely to be exposed to excessive weather conditions, the oversite concrete will be vulnerable to frost and heat damage. The best defence against frost damage is not to lay the concrete at all until the weather warms up. If this is not possible, then the area must be covered with sacking or similar fibrous sheeting material, leaving a small gap between the concrete and the covering for air flow. If the weather is hot and sunny, the concrete drying out too quickly then becomes a problem. For the best results the concrete must be kept damp for as long as possible, allowing curing to take place over two or three days. Shade from the sun is the best protection, with constant though not excessive damping down to avoid fast drying out.

Reinforced Concrete Floor

If the concrete floor is being reinforced using reinforcing sheets, then a good method is to suspend the reinforcement above the base and at a level approximately central to the floor. The concrete floor can then be poured through and around the reinforcing sheets, and this provides a very strong base. Always, when pouring oversite concrete speed is important, and a continuous flow of concrete must be achieved to allow the two floor sections to bleed together properly.

Concrete reinforcement mesh ready for concrete to be poured over.

Step by Step

- Remove all vegetative materials and topsoil from the area to be excavated.
- Carefully check the measurements and foundation positions before starting.
- Set up a datum peg from which all levels can be taken.
- Set out the foundation and finished wall positions by using profile boards.
- Make sure the foundation depth compares favourably with block and brick dimensions.
- Make a gauge rod detailing block and brick courses, lintel and finished wall levels.

- When laying 'hand-mixed' concrete ensure a constant flow to reduce the risk of joins.
- When ordering 'pre-mixed' concrete, make sure you let them know the dimensions of the area to be filled.
- When laying a hardcore oversite, make sure the materials used for the base are suitable for that purpose.
- When laying a polythene membrane, take extra care not to puncture the sheeting, and to tape any joins together properly.

CHAPTER 7

Building the Walls above the Damp Course

When all the oversite work has been completed and the walls built up to damp-proof level, the trenches can be backfilled with rubble and soil. At this stage you will have decided already the material and finish to be used for the exterior of your garage. The walls may be single skin, a single brick or block in thickness, or they may be double skin, where bricks or blocks are intertwined to form a much stronger structure. The third choice will be a cavity wall, where the building has a domestic attachment or is being prepared for future building projects.

Planning permission is often not required for a garage, so the choice of finish can be very personal, or, as is often the case, the materials chosen will be selected to match the existing dwelling. Unless you are building a sectional garage the materials you use are likely to be a straight choice between brick, block and timber. Bricks, and old bricks in particular, seldom match exactly, and where the original brickmakers no longer produce the same bricks, or are no longer in business, trying to copy the exact bricks may be difficult. When you have to choose a substitute brick it is important to consider what the effect weathering will have on it, and what the brick will look like in a few years' time. If a near match cannot be found you may decide to use a brick that you believe is complimentary to the existing bricks.

Bricks are the most popular material used in domestic building today and date back at least 5,000 years, to the Egyptians; however, they are not the only materials in use. Natural stonework, for example, dates back to long before the invention of the brick – but this extremely attractive and desirable product has become expensive to use in modern construction, and is not easy to build with. To satisfy demand and to retain appearances where existing stone buildings are common, a pre-formed, man-made block with a stone appearance is used. These blocks are less expensive, are readily available, and provide a suitable alternative to natural stone.

The use of concrete blocks with a rendered finish is also popular, even where any existing buildings are brick built. Concrete blocks are extremely heavy to build with, but they can also be very competitively priced and form a very strong structure.

BRICKLAYING

One of the oldest building trades in the business, the bricklayer is responsible for the most visible part of your new building. For this reason alone hiring an experienced, and local if possible, bricklayer is essential. The bricklayer, or 'brickie', will quote you for the job as a whole, or to carry out the work on a day-rate basis according to the degree of difficulty involved. A standard building project will generally be quoted on a fixed price, and will include setting out the walls at foundation level, building the walls, including cavity insulation, up to roof level, building in door and window frames where required, and bedding on the wall plate. The quote will not include supplying materials or plant hire, nor is it likely to include, unless otherwise agreed, making templates for window units, or erecting pole scaffolding or gable-end rafters where gable-end brickwork is involved.

A good working relationship with all the tradesmen is required, and there must be a clear understanding about what is, and is not, included in the price. All the materials must be discussed, and they must be available on site when the bricklayer arrives to start.

Mortar

In the dictionary 'mortar' is defined as a mixture of sand and cement used to join stones and bricks together. In fact it is far more important than that. A good cement mortar is essential to achieve the right finish and give lasting strength to your walls. Portland cement and soft sand at a ratio of about one part cement to four parts sand is a widely used recipe for walls both above and below ground. Non-hydraulic and semi-hydraulic lime can be added for workability and strength and to lighten the mortar, with other additives including a plasticizer for workability, and a colorant to add colour.

The mixture should not be too wet or the bricklayer will struggle to lay it as a bed for the bricks. If it is too weak (too much sand) the joints may crumble away, and if it is too strong (too much cement) the joints may crack. Enough water should be added to produce a good dropping consistency off the trowel, allowing it to spread easily and providing enough time for the brick to be laid to a line and made level. Where the bricks, the sand or the weather increase the drying out time, making life difficult for the bricklayer, a plasticizer can be added. A good bricklayer with knowledge of local sand grades will also know when the conditions are suitable for laying bricks, weatherwise, and the strength of mixture most suitable for the bricks being used.

There are three simple points for producing the best brickwork:

- Always use an experienced bricklayer.
- Keep the sand covered when it is not being used.
- Be sure always to store the cement in a dry area.

SINGLE-SKIN WALL CONSTRUCTION

Where a garage is to be dual purpose and used both to provide security and protection for a vehicle and as a workshop or store room, the walls need not be designed to retain as much heat as possible. Thus there will not be the additional costs of building a cavity wall, as single- or double-skin walls are perfectly adequate for this purpose. Single-skin walls are perfectly strong enough when they are built properly, but for added strength the wall can be built with materials producing a double thick wall. To do this the bricks, where bricks are used, can be intertwined to produce a whole variety of designs. Blocks, on the other hand, are already widely used and can easily be purchased of double thickness; some are hollow and some are solid.

Supporting materials for single- and double-skin walls including frames and lintels are also available, and must be used where appropriate to finish off the project properly. A single skin wall will be strong at the corners but fairly weak in between, and liable to become unbalanced unless intermediate piers are included.

Piers

A pier can be built in a huge variety of formats, and can be either built into the wall or free-standing. Where the pier is built into the wall it will be used either as a support for a garage door frame, or it could be a bearing for a lintel or other structural member. Where a single-skin wall extends over a length of 4m or more and there are no supporting structures abutting it or corners providing strength, then piers must be built into the wall for stability. Garages are not always subject to building regulations' approval, so it is possible to build without piers, but this can be very risky and produce a potentially unstable structure.

Where piers are to be built, the concrete foundations should be widened to include this additional bearing. Similarly where door frames – including the main garage door frame – are built, to add piers or to build a thicker wall structure will provide a better fixing point for the frame, and it

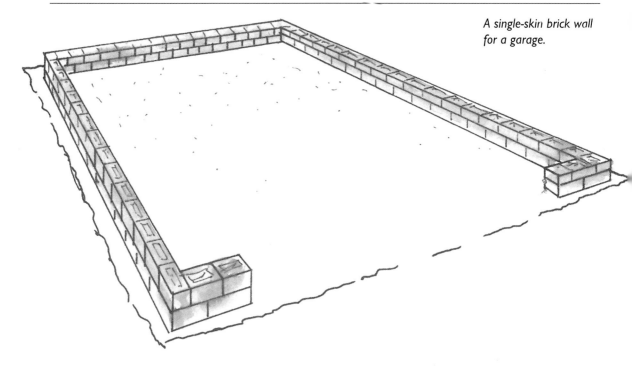

A single-skin brick wall for a garage.

Building corners to form the building shape.

A steel pier bolted to the foundation concrete slab.

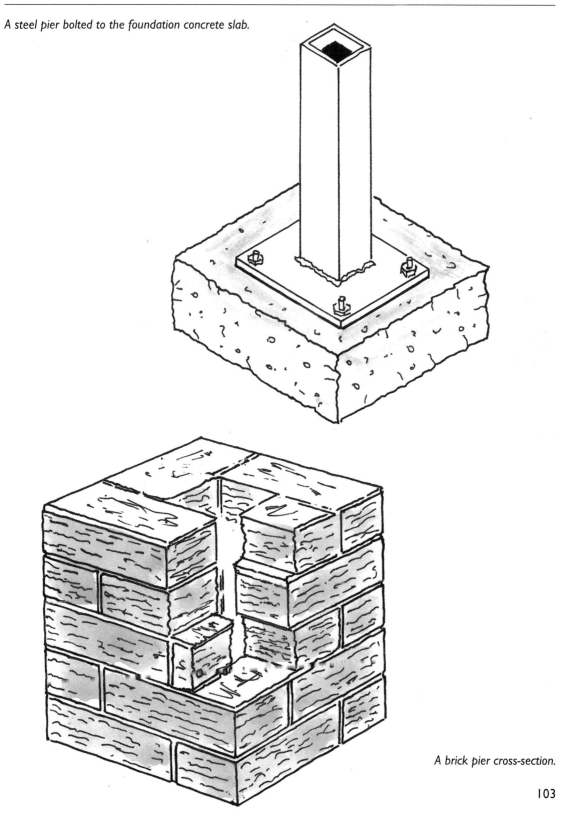

A brick pier cross-section.

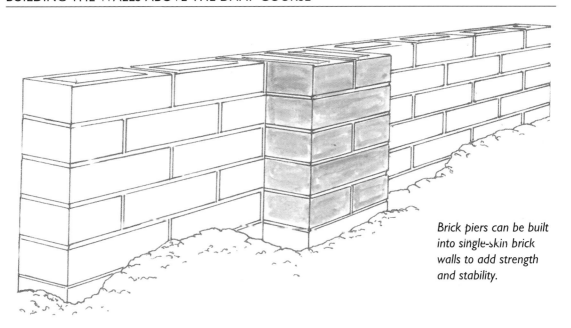

Brick piers can be built into single-skin brick walls to add strength and stability.

Piers built to the required height.

will more easily cope with the stresses and strains imposed upon it when using the door or doors.

In some cases piers will be built as free-standing structures and they should be designed for this purpose. They are more common where double and triple garages are built, with the inclusion of single garage doors as opposed to a single garage door or a double door.

CAVITY WALL CONSTRUCTION

The majority of garages are built with a single-skin wall, but where a garage is to be used for additional domestic purposes – perhaps as an annexe or utility room – then a cavity wall structure may be required for part or all of the external walls of the new building. Where this is the case the walls, windows and doors must meet with stringent building regulations requirements, and approval must be sought before building work starts. Cavity wall construction has been designed to provide protection from damp penetration and, more importantly, to reduce heat loss from the building, and consists of a decorative outer wall, a cavity filled or partially filled with an insulator, and an internal wall.

Damp penetration is one of the most serious of building defects, and can cause extensive damage to the structure, both inside and out. When a cavity wall is built properly it should not permit damp penetration, and when it does, it is usually due to the cavity being bridged, often as a result of mortar droppings left on wall ties, or mortar dropping down the cavity during construction.

The single most important factor, and where external walls must comply with current building regulations, is to reduce heat loss from the building. Every wall where windows and doors are fitted must meet accepted thermal requirements – 'U' values – from which the building's energy use can be calculated. To assist the retention of heat the internal wall can be built using insulation blocks, with more insulation added to the cavity. There are numerous variations on this theme, with the one aim of keeping energy loss to a minimum and producing a cavity wall to meet all the statutory requirements.

Cavity Wall Insulation

With fuel costs rising steadily every year, energy saving is money saving. In England and Wales there are guidelines where walls and windows must achieve a minimum in energy saving, calculated in 'U' values. The 'U' value of a wall shows the

Cavity insulation with fixings.

Cavity insulation around a window opening.

thermal transmittance (heat transfer) through a wall when outside temperatures differ from inside temperatures. To limit the heat loss through the fabric of the building, cavity wall insulation can be built into it in various forms.

Standard forms of insulation include using insulation batts 50mm thick filling the cavity, and expanded polystyrene sheets 25mm thick attached to the inner wall using special clips. Good site care is necessary to ensure that the installation process is carried out successfully. Where the cavity insulation fills the cavity, all mortar droppings should be prevented from falling down the cavity, and the insulation batts must be protected against wet weather. Where expanded polystyrene sheets are used, they must be firmly attached to the internal wall and not left flapping about freely. Installation problems may arise where the wall ties are fitted badly or irregularly, causing the slabs to be chopped about unnecessarily.

Cavity insulation built up to window-board position.

The slabs of cavity insulation will be installed by the bricklayer as he builds the walls, and the insulation must be kept clean and dry at all times. Store it in a dry place until it is used, and always cover an unfinished wall overnight as a protection against dampness.

Thermal Bridging

In recent years the insulation of domestic buildings has come a long way, but there is a weak link, around windows and doors for example, where a 'bridge' between the cold outer wall and the warm inner wall is formed. On a cold day, for instance, the warm air inside the house will travel to the colder outside air: this is called 'thermal conductivity' and is caused by a drop in temperature. It increases the risk of condensation and mould growth. For the purpose of calculating the insulation potential or the resistance of fittings in close proximity to a bridge, a chart showing the 'R' values, or resistance values, is used. Lintels are often situated in the direct vicinity of a likely thermal bridge, so to achieve the required 'R' values and to meet building regulations' requirements, they have been filled with insulation to improve their respective 'R' values. When you purchase lintels this can be accurately compared against the 'R' values of their competitors' lintels.

Where the cavity is closed in other areas – reveals around windows and doors, for example – thermal bridging products incorporating a dpc can be installed to reduce the risk of condensation and mould.

Vertical dpc
Damp penetration from the ground upwards can be prevented with the fitting of a damp-proof course. The same method of protection can be applied to window and door openings in walls. Where the external and internal walls are joined

Vertical window reveal showing vertical dpc.

together, at the 'reveals' around windows and doors, water penetration is possible so a vertical damp-proof barrier must be installed during construction as a preventative measure. An insulated cavity closer can be used, tackling both the problems of damp penetration and heat loss, through thermal bridging, at the same time.

Wall Ties
To build a stable, strong cavity wall, wall ties must be fitted at regular intervals. There are several types on the market, all designed to add strength to cavity walls in particular, and to restrict water penetration where the wall tie forms a bridge connecting the outer wall to the inner wall. Poor installation, however, where a wall tie is not level and slopes toward the inner wall, can provide the bridge necessary for rainwater, after it has soaked the outer wall, transferring the dampness to the inner wall. Your choice of wall tie may well be dictated by the type of cavity insulation you use, but with all of them the wall ties must be kept clean and free of mortar droppings during construction.

Indents and Profiles
If your new garage wall abuts the existing house wall, a proper join must be made to ensure stability. There are two principal ways of carrying out this process: the first is by cutting indents into the existing wall, forming a mortice and tenon-type joint, and then building the new wall into the indents. The second is by fixing profiles against the existing wall and building the attachments in as the wall is built. This connection will also provide a 'bridge' where dampness can penetrate through to the inside walls, so a vertical dpc must be fitted. Using a 'disc cutter' or 'angle grinder' hired from your local hire shop, you can cut a line through the wall you are building into, approximately central to the cavity of the new adjoining wall, for the full height of the building. A dpc can then be inserted, thus providing a continuous barrier against damp.

Lintels and Rolled Steel Joists (RSJs)
A lintel is a horizontal beam, originally built from stone and then formed into the shape of a brick arch, but now more commonly constructed from

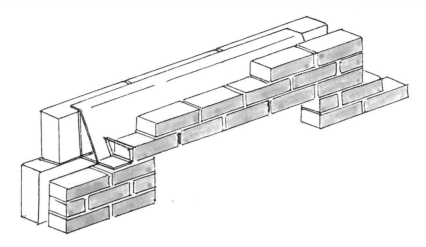

Weep vents must be inserted above lintels in cavity walls.

galvanized steel or pre-cast concrete. It provides a support for masonry above an opening such as a window or a door, and is built into the new wall as it progresses; it is bedded on mortar, with both the inner and outer walls being built up together. To function properly the lintel must be installed correctly, and should not be damaged in any way prior to its installation, as this damage may result in it failing in its task.

Building regulations specify three particular points regarding lintels:

1) The lintel must have an end bearing, resting on each supporting wall, of at least 150mm at each end.
2) The thermal bridging requirements (R values) must be achieved.
3) Water penetration, a result of water travelling down the cavity, must be directed to the external wall.

To satisfy points 2 and 3, lintel manufacturers have amended the design of their product so that the lintels are insulated to meet these requirements, and also designed like a cavity tray, to direct downward water to the outside wall. To assist this final point, additional precautions must be taken to allow this water to exit through weep holes built into the external wall at either end of the lintel; this includes the proper installation of stop ends to direct moisture towards the weep holes.

RSJs may be required to support the roof or for winch support.

An RSJ (a rolled steel joist) or a universal beam may be specified where an extra-large opening in a wall is considered outside the scope of a standard lintel. These strong beams can be purchased in a variety of lengths and cross-sections appropriate for almost any circumstance. Where a beam is required it is likely that Building Control will request structural calculations to prove the ability of the beam to carry the load to be imposed upon it. Unlike standard steel lintels, these beams can be extremely heavy, putting an extra emphasis on installation. The beam must be bedded on to special load-bearing padstones or engineering bricks, and in some cases steel plates, in order to spread an imposed load with the potential to crush standard bricks and blocks over a wider area.

DOORS AND WINDOWS

Door Frames

Door frames, with and without a sill, are commonly made from 100 x 75mm softwood with a rebate for the door. As with wooden window frames, door frames can be built into the walls as they progress. Frame ties at regular intervals, at least three each side, will anchor the frame into the mortar joints. Entrance doors, front and rear, invariably open into

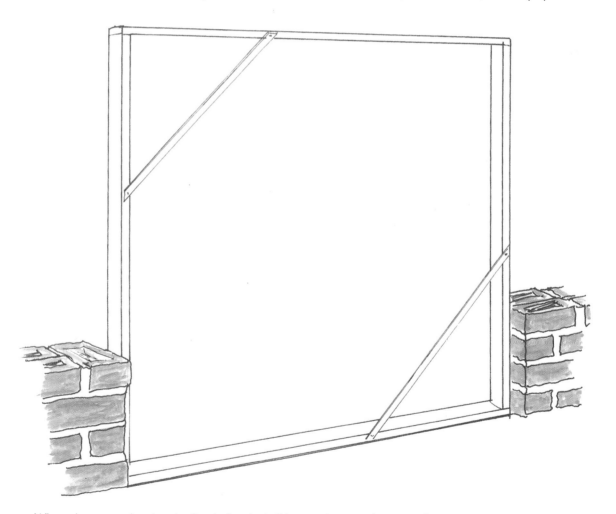

Where the garage door is to be fitted after the build a template may be required.

Building around a door opening.

the building, whilst doors opening on to a balcony or garden area will open out. To prevent rainwater penetration, a galvanized water bar will be fitted to the hardwood cill set at a point approximately central to the bottom of the door. When the door is fitted, the bottom can be rebated over the water bar as required. All timber frames should be treated or primed and undercoated before installation, with the hardwood sill doubly protected and covered against mortar or traffic damage.

Garage door frames are, by tradition, constructed from timber and securely built into the vertical jams around the opening. The garage door frame must be fitted securely to cope with the demands placed upon it by operating and by supporting heavy garage doors. A frame fitted badly and not securely will work loose and prevent the garage door or doors from operating properly. When fitted, the frame can be sealed around the edges and painted appropriately.

Not all garage doors require frames, and some have frames already fitted to them and fixed when the door is installed. Whatever you choose, please ensure the building process makes allowances for the type of door selected to prevent problems when the garage is built and the door is ready to be fitted. Alterations or amendments at this stage can be very costly and time consuming.

Other Door and Window Frames

One of the more important decisions made during the planning process would have been to select the style, size and positioning of door and window frames. The planning department will also take particular care that any windows and doors meet with their rules, which include privacy for neighbouring properties and proximity to boundaries. Building Control, on the other hand, consider windows to be a recognized source of potential problems relating to light, heat loss and ventilation. A door frame without the door will not encounter the same degree of inspection at the plans stage as that applied to windows, but there are rules for doors that must be followed, depending upon the location, and these include fire precautions.

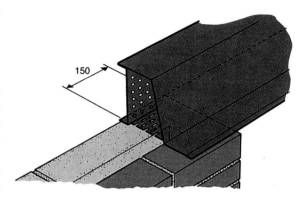

Minimum 150mm end bearings for all lintels.

The range of windows currently available from suppliers is vast, with a multitude of styles to choose from including top hung, side hung, sash and tilt windows. The glazed area of each window is important because it will let in the sunlight we require, but it will also let out heat. Double and triple glazing is available as an energy-saving option if required. New bathrooms and toilets attract the closest inspection, where you will find ventilation is high on the list of priorities. Building regulations stipulate a minimum area of window opening for any habitable room to be at least one-twentieth of that room's floor area plus background ventilation, with a proportion of the primary ventilation at least 1.75m above floor level.

Background ventilation, generally fitted to windows in the shape of a trickle vent, will provide a source of constant and additional ventilation as an aid to reducing the risk of condensation.

Unglazed Window Frames

It is standard building practice for the bricklayer to build unglazed window frames into walls as they progress. Before installation, wooden frames, including freshly sawn areas, should be stained or painted with primer and undercoated, then covered with sheeting as a protection against mortar damage. Frame ties – galvanized or stainless steel are the most common – will be screwed into the frames at regular intervals and then bedded into the mortar joints as the walls are built.

A typical window opening.

Window Templates

Building new 'made-to-measure' windows, with the glazing installed, into the walls as they progress can be a very risky practice with a serious possibility of damage. The best and most popular solution to this problem is to make, or get your carpenter to make, templates for the bricklayer to build the new walls around. The templates can then be removed and discarded, and the new windows installed when all the construction work is completed. Each template can be made according to the size specified by your window manufacturer – but a strong word of caution: the templates must be accurate, as trying to fit a window into an opening too small for it can pose massive unwanted difficulties.

Right: A scaffold plank offers excellent support to a template.

Above: Window and door templates supported during the build.

Door template resting on the damp-proof course.

SCAFFOLDING

The technical term used in the trade when refer-ring to the height of walls during construction is the 'lift', and a 'lift' is a height at which scaffolding is required for tradesmen such as bricklayers to work from. For example, when a wall reaches the first 'lift' height the bricklayer will require scaffold-ing to stand on so that the building can be built up to the next 'lift'. Similarly, when the walls are built up to the second 'lift', then a further level is required to put the roof on.

The scaffolding referred to in this example is called 'pole' scaffolding where poles, or stand-ards, are raised vertically, and lateral poles, called ledgers, are bolted on horizontally. There are two types of pole scaffolding commonly in use: the first is a 'putlog' scaffold where special short poles with one end flattened off, called putlogs, are built into the walls as a support for the planks the builders will work off. The whole scaffold is then braced at regular intervals through openings in the wall, windows for example, for stability.

The second type of pole scaffold is an 'inde-pendent' scaffold, an almost freestanding scaffold, where two rows of standards are raised vertically then bolted together with ledgers. This second type may appear to be freestanding, but all scaffold must be tied into the building at regular intervals. Pole scaffolding of this type must be erected by highly skilled professionals as there are very stringent safety measures to abide by.

Scaffold Hire

The height of the finished building works will determine the type of scaffold required for the work to be carried out safely and successfully. If the height is less than 8ft (2.4m), then trestles

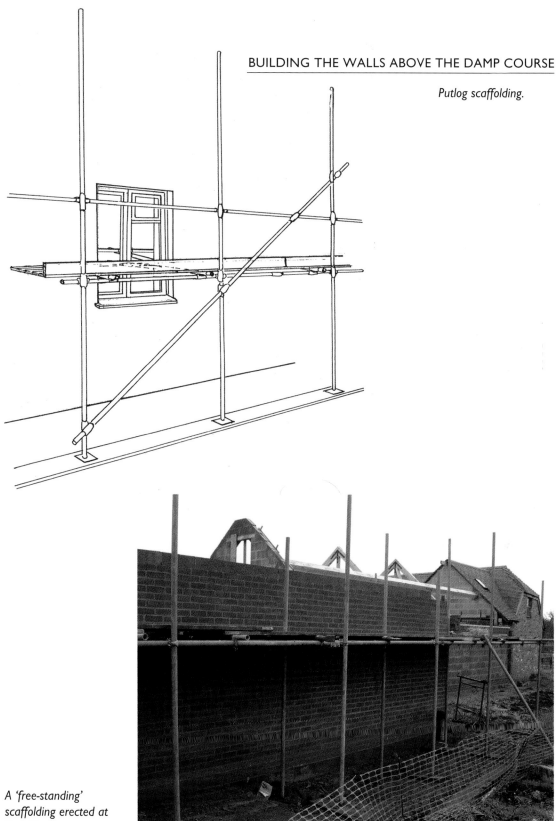

Putlog scaffolding.

A 'free-standing'
scaffolding erected at
first lift.

Ladders must be set at a suitable angle and tied to the scaffolding to avoid accidents.

and planks are an option: these can be hired from your local hire shop and erected by the bricklayer during construction. If the extension height exceeds 2.4m, or if the tradesmen request it, then pole scaffolding is likely to be the safest option.

Professional supply and fit scaffolders are essential, and they can be found in your local *Yellow Pages*. They will quote you for scaffolding the whole project, including additional lifts, then deliver and erect the lifts as required. Needless to say, liaising closely with the scaffolders and the tradesmen will go a long way to ensuring that the project can continue without delays.

THE WALL PLATES

When the walls are built up to roof level, a 100 x 50mm softwood wall plate will be fitted, to rest the roof timbers on and secure the roof to. In the majority of cases the wall plate will be bedded on the inner wall and then secured with mild steel galvanized restraint straps set at a maximum of 2m centres, and starting no more than 450mm from corners. To ensure that the roof can be built geometrically, the wall plates, bedded on to opposite walls, must be level and squared with each other.

Step by Step

- Make sure the materials you use compliment the existing property.
- When using cavity wall insulation ensure it is stored in a dry building and that it is protected from inclement weather during construction.
- Cover sand over when it is not in use, and store cement in a dry building.
- Make sure lintels have a minimum 150mm end bearing.
- A vertical damp-proof course should be fitted around all wall openings.
- The wall plate should be secured at regular intervals to the new walls.
- Always employ experienced and qualified tradesmen.
- Make sure all safety measures are in place when working from, and erecting, scaffolding.

CHAPTER 8

Constructing the Roof

To many observers the completion of a roof will constitute the end of the serious building work, but in fact there is still some way to go, and the ground-workers, bricklayers and roofers will be replaced by the finishing tradesmen. True, the completed roof construction will generally signal an end to all the 'major' building works, leaving an enclosed building structure partially protected from the elements. Works that include excavations, drainage and walls will be finished, or nearly so – but where one trade reaches its conclusion, another will start, commencing a completely new section of the project. The finishing trades may include floor layers, plasterers, electricians, plumbers and others, and these may well take at least the same, if not more, time to bring the project to its completion.

From a tradesman's point of view there is likely to be a change of personnel as the carpenter replaces the bricklayer to complete the roofing framework, and then the roofer replaces the carpenter to make the building watertight. At this stage it is important that any handover from one trade to another goes smoothly, and the building is built properly and professionally, the completed new walls square and level and the timbers set to receive the roof structure firmly secured to the new walls. All equipment should be in proper working order, scaffolding should be stable, with all the scaffold boards secure and fully supported, and the proper safety measures should be observed.

When preparations are made for the roof to be fitted, the carpenter will soon discover how square the building is and how level the wall plates are. For simple roofs such as a flat roof the variations may not be too difficult to overcome or even to live with, but for more complicated roofs – hipped roofs are a prime example – a building out of square could prove to be disastrous, and very expensive to rectify.

FLAT ROOF CONSTRUCTION

Historically the flat roof, now extremely common in single-storey buildings, has been widely used in Middle Eastern countries for many centuries where the climate is dry and arid. But it wasn't until the nineteenth century and the introduction of more advanced waterproofing techniques that the flat roof became more widely used in Europe. The popularity of flat roofs, possibly the simplest of all roofs to install on single-storey buildings, has not been continued through the building regulations approvals process to buildings above one storey. That is not to say approval is never obtained, but it is particularly uncommon.

Building a flat roof structure is not a difficult building process and should fall easily within the remit of a competent do-it-yourself enthusiast. To start with, the flat roof will consist of a row of timber joists, with firring strips attached, resting on and secured to the wall plates. Decking sheets will be laid on top of the new joists, with a tilt fillet attached along the perimeters, followed by layers of bitumen felt built up and laid hot on to the sheet decking to provide a secure waterproof covering.

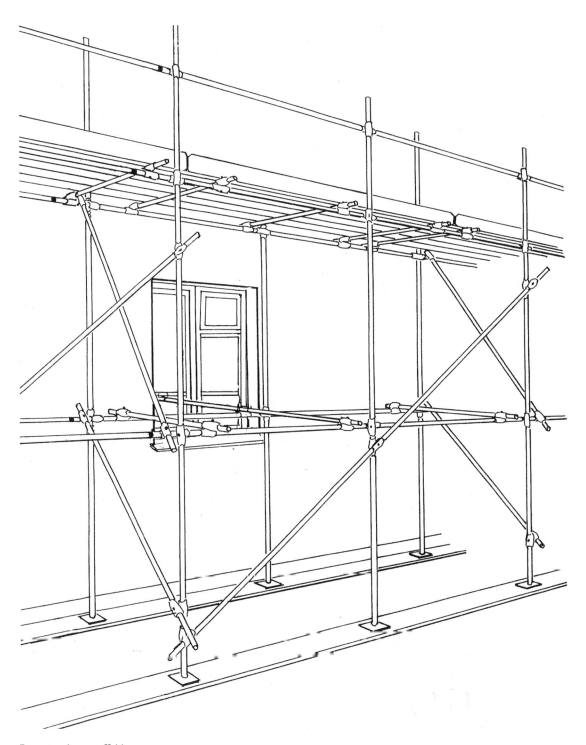

Free-standing scaffolding.

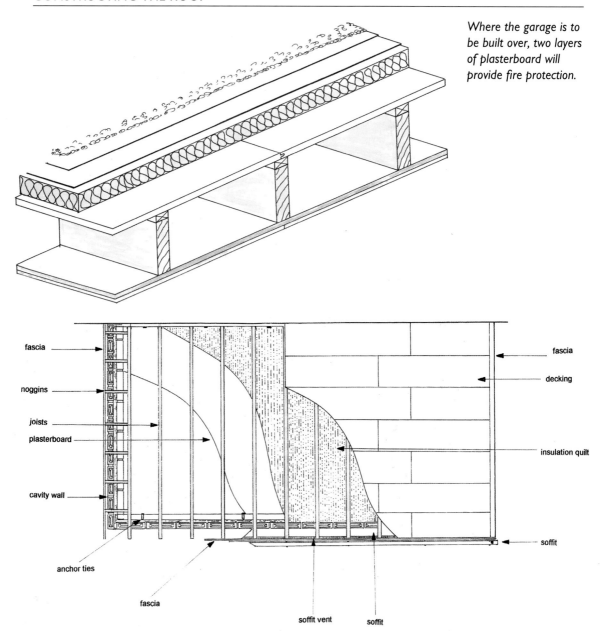

Where the garage is to be built over, two layers of plasterboard will provide fire protection.

A typical flat roof layout.

Flat Roof Insulation

In standard garage construction with single-skin walls and simple roof structure there may be little need to insulate the roof area; however, a garage can now be designed and built for more purposes than the storage of vehicles, so details of roofing insulation have been included. Whether the insulation is laid on top of, or between the joists, to ensure that the structure achieves the energy-saving requirements necessary to comply with building regulations, will be clearly specified on the building plans.

A 'cold' roof where the insulation is fitted between the joists.

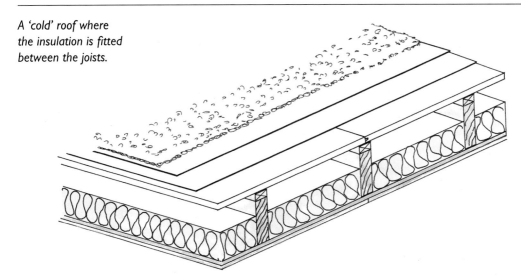

In flat roof construction there are two distinctive types of flat roof: a 'cold' roof and a 'warm' roof. The 'cold' roof is constructed in the usual way, only with the roof insulation fitted in the roof void 'between' the roof joists and with the decking above and the ceiling boards below. The void must not be completely filled with insulation otherwise condensation will gather and cause damage to the ceiling boards. To avoid condensation problems occurring in cold roofs the void, the area between the joists, must be ventilated (see illustrations) with a clear airflow above the insulation and below the flat roof decking. The free airflow created in the void area is designed to avoid and prevent condensation gathering, and will be assisted by ventilation gaps strategically placed along the side edges of the roof.

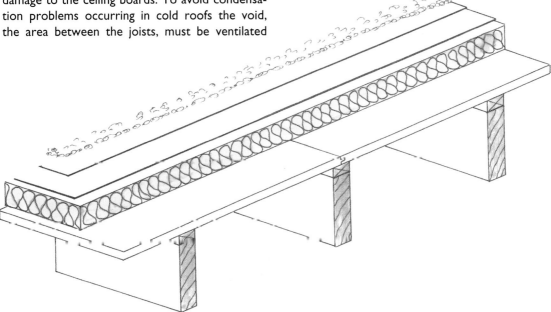

A 'warm' roof where the insulation is laid above the joists.

A 'warm' roof is constructed with the insulation built in between the bitumen felt waterproof covering and a vapour barrier fixed to the roof decking. This construction will leave the void area between the flat roof and the ceiling boards completely free, and will be ventilated in the same way as the cold roof.

Flat Roof Joists

The timber joists, spanning from one wall to either an opposite wall or other agreed and approved support, will be laid level and at the centres specified on the approved building plans, ready for the flat roof decking to be attached. Before placing an order for the roofing joists there are three important factors to take into consideration: the size, the grade and the length. The joist sizes 150 x 50mm, 175 x 50mm and 200 x 50mm are the most common, but the actual size required will be clearly specified on your building plans.

The grade, or strength of the timber, may also be specified on the building plans, and will be one of three common grades of timber used for this type of construction: general stress (GS) grade, special stress (SS) grade and machine general stress (MGS) grade. The GS and SS grades are graded and assessed visually, noting the grain and the position of knots, whereas the MGS grade is assessed mechanically to ensure that it is suitable and meets the requirements for this grade.

The length of the joists required could easily be taken from the plans, but it is advisable to measure

Timber spacers fitted between joists.

the lengths required from the actual building itself, always allowing for, and adding a little extra length for, tolerances and installation.

Generally each roofing joist will be fitted on to the wall plate at a specified 'centre' as shown on the building plans. The 'centre' measurement is taken from the centre of one joist to the centre of the adjacent joists, and so on (see illustration). You may reduce the centres of the joists to more easily accommodate the decking sheets, and reduce the amount of cutting where required, but it is not advisable to increase the centres of the joists without prior and detailed discussion with the building inspector.

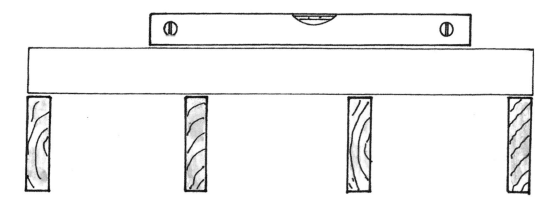

When laying joists make sure they are level.

A restraint strap securing the wall plate in position.

Restraint straps at good intervals.

The size or dimension of the timber required for the roof joists will be calculated from approved charts when the plans are being prepared. The dimension of the joists, for example 200 x 50mm, will be determined by the length of the span of the joist, from one supporting wall to the opposite supporting wall, or other approved support. With this 'span' measurement and from the load likely to be imposed upon the joists – in this case the weight of the felt roof itself, and any further imposed loads placed upon the roof, snow for example – the size of the joists can be calculated fairly accurately.

Restraint Straps

When the roofing joists are in position and firmly secured to the wall plate, mild steel restraint straps can and should be fitted in specified locations to ensure the roof does not move or flap around in strong winds. Restraint straps are very important in garage structures where the equivalent of one wall, where the door is fitted, can be wide open to the elements and therefore strong gusts of wind.

The restraint straps will need to be fitted in specified locations according to and as shown on the building plans, and spaced out at approximately 2m centres, and a strap must be placed within 450mm of every corner of the building. The restraint straps will first be securely fixed to a joist and will then extend down the wall for at least 1m. These straps will then be firmly secured to the wall with at least four fixings. Galvanized nails or screws are recommended, with the bottom fixing no more than 150mm from the bottom of the restraint strap.

Firring section

A flat roof is a slightly misleading term, because in fact the roof is not really flat at all: if it were, then rainwater damage would reduce its life substantially. To provide the necessary slope a flat roof requires, and to direct the rainwater away and into the gutters, a firring piece will need to be fitted to each joist before the decking sheets are laid. A firring piece is a strip of timber of generally the same width as the roof joist, and will provide a fall, or slope, on the roof of at least one in forty. The firring pieces can be ordered from your supplier to the dimensions you require.

Dealing with Condensation

In standard garage structures where the roof void is not enclosed condensation will not be a problem, but where the building forms part of a domestic structure then the effects of condensation may well need to be considered. Condensation is an action we are all well aware of, and is formed where hot air meets cooler air with very little in the way of ventilation between them – in the roof void, for example. Large quantities of condensation are produced in the average modern home from cooking, taking a bath and having a shower. Even breathing and perspiring produce condensation. This warm, moist air will be drawn by convection to parts of the building where the air is cooler. Modern homes are now so very well

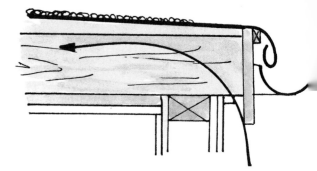

Flat roof ventilation.

insulated in walls and windows that the roof void is left as a very vulnerable area. Once the warm air has entered the roof void, condensation can occur. Cross-ventilation of this area will remove the warm air before damaging condensation can occur.

Cross-Ventilation

To reduce the risk of damage to timbers and roof fixings and ceiling boards as a direct result of condensation, and to prevent mould growth within the roof void, an effective roof ventilation system is required and should be specified on the building plans. Free air must be allowed to flow from one side of the roof to the other without interruption above the layer of insulation and below the flat roof decking. To achieve this, a gap at least 50mm wide will be left between the roof insulation and the roof decking, and this will provide a good space for ventilation over the bulk of the roof, supported by continuous ventilation along the eaves. This continuous ventilation will be provided by openings along opposite sides of the roof. The openings can be a continuous gap along the eaves where eaves ventilators can be fitted, or alternatively circular eaves ventilators can be fixed into the soffit board (see illustration).

Whichever system you choose, the combined areas of the opening must be equivalent to a continuous gap of 25mm running the full length of the eaves. Where the openings run in the same direction as the roof joists, notches can be cut into the firring pieces at regular intervals to aid cross-ventilation.

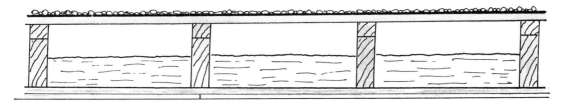

A flat roof section with insulation installed.

Flat Roof Decking

For a 'cold' roof, sheets of exterior grade plywood or tongued-and-grooved chipboard will be laid on top of the roofing joists to provide a secure and stable 'deck' to receive the layers of roofing felt and hot bitumen. If you are building a 'warm' roof, then the insulation will be laid on top of the decking sheets ready to receive the layers of roofing felt and hot bitumen.

With the roof joists in position and centred to reduce any wastage caused by having to cut the decking boards, the decking can be nailed to the roof joists using galvanized nails. The thickness of the plywood or chipboard sheets you use will be determined by the space between the joists, and will be specified on the building plans.

When using chipboard sheeting, try to reduce the time the sheets are exposed to the weather by

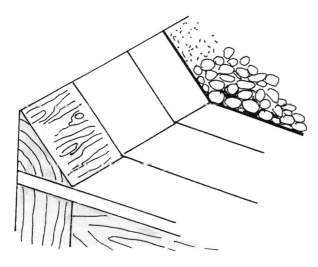

Flat roof tilt fillet.

ensuring the sheets are fitted immediately prior to the felt roof installation.

The Tilt Fillet

A tilt fillet is a triangular shaped piece of timber used around the perimeters of flat roofs to provide a guide for and to ensure that rainwater is deflected into the gutters. The tilt fillet will be nailed to the decking, along the edges and around the perimeters of the roof where required. The bitumen felt roofing will be dressed over the tilt fillet, and finished off with a layer of mineral felt for appearances and for protection from the rays of the sun.

Felt Roofing

Asphalt, bitumen-based waterproofing methods have been in use for many centuries; records can be found as far back as the rebuilding of Babylon, and more recently – at least 200 years ago – it was applied to ships' timbers to make them waterproof and more seaworthy. A natural product, asphalt can be produced from limestone rocks and shale, and in some areas is found in a liquid form. This natural asphalt is not found in the UK, but is common in areas of France, Switzerland and Germany where asphalt-impregnated limestone is mined. The largest natural liquid form asphalt deposit can be found in Trinidad: known as Trinidad Asphalt Lake, it has a consistency almost dense enough to walk on.

Recent years have seen great improvements in the durability of asphalt, resulting in widespread usage throughout the building industry. Mastic asphalt and bitumen-based roofing felt have been combined to produce a highly efficient and commonly used waterproof membrane for flat roofs in particular. The built-up bitumen roof, the most popular form of multi-layer roofing, has gone through rigorous testing over recent years, with the result that, in the UK, a British Standard CP 144 Part 4, covering the application of mastic asphalt roofing, and BS 747, covering bitumen-based roofing felts, are being enforced.

There are two forms of built-up roof: the first is used on cold roofs and the second on warm roofs. When applying a built-up bitumen roof covering to a cold roof, the first layer of felt is secured to the deck using hot bitumen or large-headed galvanized nails, followed by at least two layers of felt bonded in hot bitumen. Importantly, the additional layers must have staggered joints, with an overlap of at least 50mm where joints occur.

To finish off, a layer of reflective mineral felt will be fitted to exposed areas and a layer of reflective stone chippings will be bedded in bitumen to protect the roof from the effects of ultraviolet radiation.

For a 'warm' roof the waterproof covering is laid on top of the insulation, but first a vapour barrier must be bedded on top of the decking for the insulation to be laid on. A perforated layer of felt is then laid on top of the insulation with hot bitumen poured over the top, sealing it to the insulation through the perforations. A top layer, as with the cold roof, is bedded on, and then the process is finished in the same way as with a cold roof. It is important to avoid walking, or any traffic movement at all, on the completed roof as this will cause punctures and eventually result in a breakdown of the waterproof membrane.

Herringbone Struts

To stabilize any timber joists, and flat roof joists in particular, a row of herringbone struts will be installed midway along the length of the joist. These struts will help produce a really secure structure, whether plasterboards are fitted or not. If, however, the span exceeds 4m, two rows of struts may be required. The struts can be cut from timber, or they can be bought from the supplier and securely nailed in place.

Where the joist run ends adjacent to a wall,

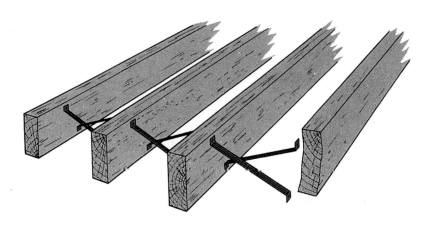

'Catnic' herringbone struts.

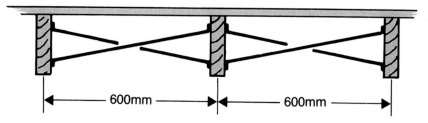

Joists at 600mm centres with herringbone struts.

600mm — 600mm

for example, timber wedges can be installed to provide an overall and continuous rigidity to the whole floor.

THE PITCHED ROOF

Although more complex and better designed to meet the challenges of various climates, roof coverings have changed very little during the last one thousand years. In fact ever since man left his cave and lived in the portable structures commonly seen and still in use in some parts of Africa, simple roof coverings became essential. A sloping roof originally made from branches covered with dead plants and grasses has steadily progressed into the thatched and tiled roof we know and love today. Clay tiles, previously hand made and dating as far back as the thirteenth century, were used to cover roofs in areas where suitable clay was found, eventually replacing the thatched roof as the primary roof covering. Now machine made, clay tiles can be seen in numerous shapes, sizes and colours throughout the country and all around the world.

The roof structure, flat or pitched, has also progressed, with a mass of building regulations set in place to ensure that it is strong enough to carry the load imposed upon it, well insulated to assist energy conservation, and ventilated to prevent damage from condensation. Add to this the roof's appearance and how it compares, contrasts and compliments the existing building, and you will immediately realize how multi-functional a roof is

now designed to be. Of course the choice of roof shape and possible covering for your own building project may be just a copy or simple duplication of the existing dwelling roof. Even the slope may be set at the same angle for aesthetic purposes. Whatever you decide upon, whether a steeper or a shallower roof, the important factor to bear in mind is 'does this new roof complement the existing roof?' If not, then perhaps a suitable and complementary alternative can be found.

PITCHED ROOF CONSTRUCTION

What is a 'pitched' roof? A roof is classified as a pitched roof when the pitch or slope exceeds 10 degrees, though the design of acceptable roof coverings for domestic buildings dictates that the slope is more likely to be in excess of $17\frac{1}{2}$ degrees.

A pitched roof is a construction configured using rafters and ceiling joists in general and forming an 'A'-shaped structure. The range of possibilities, and covering the majority of choices, will include lean-to roofs, close-coupled roofs and the less popular mono-pitched roof. The most common and widely used construction for domestic building works is the 'cut' roof, formed on site by the carpenter. Working from dimensions and specifications taken from the approved building plans and measurements taken on site, the carpenter will build the new roof from timbers cut to length to form rafters and joists. The timber dimensions will be specified on the building plans, but the timber lengths for the rafters and joists will not. At this point it may be advisable to consult with the carpenter before placing orders for timber. The carpenter will know what allowances to make for angles and overhangs.

The second choice of roof construction is the use of truss rafters. A truss rafter is a machine-made roof member of rafters and ceiling joists, now very common in domestic construction. It is structurally designed by the manufacturer and made to suit your particular requirements. Truss rafters are almost always much easier to install than a 'cut' roof, and reduce labour costs quite considerably. However, the cost of buying truss

Truss rafters resting on the wall plate.

rafters, especially in a small quantity, can be significantly higher for smaller domestic building projects such as home extensions, conversions and garages because only a few trusses are likely to be required. Even so, you may want to weigh up the cost of materials and labour of a 'cut' roof in order to compare it accurately with the cost of a truss roof, including labour to fit it. It is likely your local builder's merchant or timber supplier will provide you with a quotation for the trusses you require, and then you will need a carpenter to quote you for the labour involved.

Whichever roof structure you choose, whether a 'cut' roof or roof trusses, when the timbers arrive on site they must be stored on a flat and level surface and in a dry place until they are required for use.

LEAN-TO ROOF AND MONO PITCHED ROOF

A lean-to roof is exactly what it says: it leans against another building, from which it gets support. A lean-to roof will also have a single pitch or slope away from the structure providing the support.

A mono pitched roof is also self explanatory, in that it has a single slope or pitch.

CLOSE-COUPLED ROOF

A close-coupled roof has a double pitch, and is where two rafters are fixed to a ridge board at the top of the slope and the wall plates, secured to opposite walls, at the end of the slope. A ceiling joist or similar horizontal joist spans from wall plate to wall plate, and is secured to the rafters to prevent them from spreading apart. The horizontal joists can be set at different heights depending upon the design, but are used for the purpose of forming the 'A'-frame shape so common in close-coupled roofs.

Larger variations of a close-coupled roof include purlins positioned mid-way along the rafters. Purlins are used to increase the span of the rafters without increasing the size of the timber required. Timber struts may also be specified and positioned where possible to help direct the load imposed on the roof down to a load-bearing point.

Rafters secured to wall plate.

Roof timbers with spacers fitted for stability.

Roof timbers with struts added for additional support.

Binders to help tie the whole structure together and prevent a collapse, and hangers supporting the joists, will provide combined and increased support to ceiling joists and rafters.

A Gable Ladder

Where the roof overlaps a gable-end wall, a support will be required for the overhanging tiles. If the overhang is small, then a rafter may be fitted on the outside of the wall structure to support the roof overhang. However, when the overhang exceeds 150mm, then a gable ladder may be needed to cope with the overhanging tile weight. A gable ladder is called a 'ladder' because of its appearance, it looks like a ladder, and it will be made using the final internal rafter adjoining a similar rafter set externally.

The barge boards and soffit are fitted to provide the decorative covering.

Fascia, Soffit and Barge Boards

The decorative timber facings around the perimeter of a roof all fulfil a role. The vertical timber attached to the rafter ends along the eaves, providing a good clean finish and for attaching the guttering to, is the fascia. Set to 'kick up' the last line of tiles and to provide a drip over which water will run from the roof into the guttering, a fascia board can be found on the majority of modern homes built today. Underneath, but attached to the fascia, is a soffit. The soffit closes off any entrance to the roof void between the overhanging rafters, keeping out birds and flying insects while providing ventilation to the roof void by way of soffit vents fitted to the soffit at specified intervals. A soffit can be made in timber sheet such as plywood, or masterboard-type materials.

The barge boards are similar to the fascia boards in that they are fitted generally for decorative purposes and are attached to the gable-end timbers. The barge boards will be fitted to run up the slope of the roof, providing a support for any verge tiles overlapping the roof's edge. The fascia and barge boards can be made from 25mm thick timbers and painted, or from specially designed plastic UPVC to reduce maintenance costs.

Felt and Batten

Roof timbers ready to be felted.

Felt and batten to verges.

Drape felt into the guttering position.

Fitted to the rafters to provide the first waterproof covering is the roofing or sarking felt; it provides a secondary protection to the roof area from wind-driven rain and snow. Roofing felt should be made from an untearable fabric and be suitable for this purpose. To prevent water travelling down the roofing felt and into the roof void, an overlap of at least 100mm must be allowed where one layer of roofing felt joins another, down the slope of the roof. Secure joints around openings formed for soil vent pipes, for example, must be formed. The roofing felt is secured at eaves level, and additional strips are added to over-hip and under-valley areas.

Softwood roofing battens, pre-treated with a preservative, secure the roofing felt in place, and where battens are joined or abutted, the smallest length of batten should span a minimum of at least three rafters. Roofing batten sizes are generally 32 x 19mm for rafters up to 450mm centres, and 32 x 25mm for rafters up to 600mm centres. The nails or fixings used should be galvanized or similarly protected from water damage, and must be appropriate for this purpose.

Roof Tiles

Concrete, slate or clay interlocking pantiles and plain tiles form the majority of roof coverings, and are now available in a huge variety of styles and colours. The plain tile in clay and concrete is slightly cambered to assist water discharge off the roof and into gutters. Specially made tiles called 'tile and a half' tiles can be used to make sure roof tiles can be staggered on alternating rows, thus producing a more secure and waterproof covering for the roof. These should be inserted at the verges on alternating rows.

Another specially designed tile is the verge tile. Verge tiles can be inserted along the eaves to help support the fall and direct all rainwater into the guttering. Valley tiles are pre-formed in a wide variety of styles and sizes, and can be used to form the valleys where one roof abuts another.

To finish off the roof, hip tiles forming hips on hipped roofs and ridge tiles to be used along ridges are also among the list of special tiles available in a huge variety of shapes to complete the roof covering.

Load out the roof with the tiles to be laid.

Working towards the verge area.

A well finished verge.

Tiles and felt to carry rainwater into the guttering.

The verge tiles can be cemented in to finish off.

Roof Slates

Slates, both natural and manufactured, are not as common as the clay and concrete tiles on modern houses, but are still in use in most areas, particularly the older-style cottages and houses. Slate is very hard wearing and durable and can be bought in a variety of colours. Each slate is secured in place by copper or galvanized nails, with an overlap covering the nail heads. As with tiles, the first row of slates is covered by a second row with a half slate stagger, providing a half bond to reduce wind damage and to retain waterproofing. A slate roof can be a lighter roof than a tiled roof, so more slates may be required to cover the area of the roof.

Ridge and hip slates are often seen in clay, and sometimes of a different colour than the roof slates, to provide a clear outline to the roof.

Fitting the Guttering

While the scaffolding is still *in situ*, and after the roof covering is completed, the rainwater guttering can be fitted. There is a wide range and variety of styles and colours of guttering to choose from,

varying from cast iron to plastic to aluminium. Garage guttering can be obtained in a smaller dimension than standard domestic guttering, but in the main it is likely that you will use a gutter identical to the existing property. Gutter brackets to support the gutter channel should be set at approximately 900mm centres, as applicable for standard domestic conditions, with downpipe brackets set at 2m centres. These measurements are for guidance purposes only, and site conditions plus details shown on the building plans will hold sway. It is worth noting that this may be a good time to decorate the fascia boards and other timbers, while the scaffolding is still there and before the guttering is fitted. Good planning at this stage will save both time and money later on.

Carpentry Work

Constructing a pitched roof on site is not a job for the inexperienced, although garage roofs may not be as complicated as those for general domestic buildings. However, it is always wise to use the most experienced tradesmen you can get in, as any extra cost is likely to be offset by the quality of the work. Snug-fitting joints at the ridge and eaves levels, bird's mouth fittings at wall plate level, not to mention the additional work involved with a hipped roof, will assist the strength and stability of the new roof structure.

Also at this time there may be a lot of supplementary work for the carpenter to do, including fascia, soffit and barge board fitting. And when the roof is completed, the carpenter can fit the guttering while the scaffolding is still in place. Before any work is carried out by tradesmen be sure to get a fixed price for every item of work required. Extra work may be very expensive if a price has not been agreed before the work commences.

QUOTATIONS

The carpenter, along with any other tradesman, will normally quote to do this section of work on one of two schemes. The first and most common within the building industry is known as 'price work'. From the drawings showing the work required, a price to complete the work can be calculated and is submitted for acceptance. It may be broken down into separate phases of work, or it may be a total price for the completed work. It is likely that the work quoted for will not include bedding on the wall plates because this is the responsibility of the bricklayer. However, it will include, unless otherwise specified, stripping back where a new roof abuts an existing roof for valleys to be formed, and fitting fascias and soffit. As stated in an earlier section, the carpenter may also be the best person to fit the guttering, though this will not generally be included in the price given.

The second method of employment for the carpenter is a 'day rate' basis. This method is not

A good, clean roof finish.

commonly used for standard domestic building work, but is more applicable to difficult conversion works. On a day rate basis the carpenter will agree a price to be paid per day, and what work is to be carried out on a day rate basis. He will then expect to be paid at the end of each week for the days completed.

The carpenter will work on a 'labour only' basis; it is unlikely he will work on a 'supply and fix' basis, where the tradesman supplies all the materials and charges for them as the job goes along. The roof tiler, however, may work on a supply and fix basis, and these details will be clearly shown on the quotation given.

Larger roof-tiling businesses will always offer supply and fix rates for the job. By doing this they can ensure all the materials and fixings are on site when their workers arrive, and there are few hold-ups. This method may seem to be expensive at first sight of the quotation, but it will reduce the risk of over-ordering and wastage. It is also not unusual, in these instances, for a small deposit to be requested by the company for the materials supplied.

If, on the other hand, you are quite happy to supply all the materials and you want a labour only price, make sure this is clearly understood from the outset. The labour price will include laying all the roofing felt, fitting the roof battens and fixing the tiles, forming any valleys required and bedding on the verge and ridge tiles.

Where lead valleys and flashings are being fitted, make sure the roofer knows that this is part of the work quoted for. Smaller domestic projects completed in a few days will generally require a single payment when the work is completed satisfactorily.

CHAPTER 9

Garage Doors

It is important to choose the garage door you prefer before the garage plans have been prepared because the style, function and operating room required must all be decided at an early stage. With so many garage doors available 'off the peg', these dimensions should be included on the building plans. Custom-made doors can be produced where sizes do not meet the standard sizes available, but these doors will be more expensive, and ordering time must be allowed in order to prevent delays on the build. There is a very wide range and variety of garage doors available to satisfy today's discerning consumer, and the only difficulty will be making the final decision and selecting one to meet your every requirement. And there is also the option available to design the door or doors personally to give them that individual touch.

If you live on an estate where garage doors are nearly all of standard design, the choice is quite simple. And of course, do not forget that there may also be local authority planning department stipulations in place stating that any new garage doors must be identical to, or compare favourably with, existing doors, thus reducing the choice even more. If, however – and this is more likely – the choice is yours, then the boundaries are almost limitless. With today's market solutions, and companies eager and ready to produce doors from a wide range of materials and an even wider range of styles, then finding the door or doors of your choice should be fairly easy. The function may be relatively straightforward considering there are only doors that open up and down or in and out. And the widest range of all will be colour. To help with the selection process we will carefully consider each point.

THE SELECTION PROCESS

The following are examples of the types of door that suit different garages:

- A single garage with a front opening for one vehicle can be fitted with a standard up-and-over door, a roller door that rolls upwards into the roof area, or two side-hung doors opening in or outwards.
- A double garage with one single opening wide enough for two vehicles side by side can be fitted with a large, standard up-and-over door, a roller door, or two single side-hung doors.
- A double garage with two front openings each for one vehicle can be fitted with any combination of up-and-over door, roller door or side-hung doors.

Three important points should be considered before selecting the garage door: security, location, and the weather.

- Depending upon the area you live in, the door may need additional security features over and above the existing lock; it may need to be extra sturdy as well.
- Is the garage prominent, easily seen and accessible, or is it secluded, out of sight and not easily accessible? These points may well determine how the structure works in practice.

Timber up-and-over garage door.

- And finally, if the garage entrance door or doors are north facing and therefore likely to be battered on occasions by inclement weather, then ensure they can cope in both the short and the long term.

Choose a door suitable for your location.

CONSTRUCTION MATERIAL

When you have decided the type of garage door you require, you will then need to decide what material it should be constructed from.

Steel: Almost certainly the most economical choice. Galvanized steel is used for garage doors, to protect them from inclement weather and steel doors are singularly the most common garage door available on the market today. They are available in single, double and even triple layer construction, and can be insulated for energy efficiency and noise reduction.

Aluminium: Has several advantages over steel in that doors are lighter and therefore cause less wear and tear on mechanisms. The lighter weight makes handling easier for the user, and doors have a significantly greater weather resistance than those made in either steel or wood. Aluminium doors can also be insulated for energy saving and noise resistance.

Wood: Has become less popular in the garage door market due mainly to its high maintenance and shorter life expectancy. Side-hung wooden doors do, however, still offer an advantage in size or dimensions. They can be made to a wide variety of widths and height that restricts the up-and-over models, and there is no need for roller door storage or electrical motor installations.

Wooden doors can be very high on maintenance and need to be kept well painted, according to manufacturers' instructions, to reduce weather damage.

Steel up-and-over garage door.

Attractively designed garage doors for all locations.

Composite wooden doors are doors constructed using compressed and recycled wood fibres. These doors are more weather resistant than old-fashioned wooden doors, and are energy efficient.

ABS: A tough, durable material that complements UPVC and is virtually impact and dent resistant. The doors are maintenance free, and are both strong and light in weight.

STYLE

When you have decided the material you would prefer the door to be constructed from, you will need to decide which style will suit your garage best. There are generally five different garage door styles:

Retractable: An up-and-over operation, and swings completely into the garage roof area.

Canopy: Also an up-and-over door, but unlike the retractable door a good proportion of the door remains outside the garage, forming, as its name implies, a canopy.

Timber-framed garage with roller door.

Insulated roller door.

Sectional: Travels vertically, operating within the garage where its sectional make-up requires less operational space than the up-and-over doors.

Roller: Requires less operating space than other doors, and retracts into a roll often immediately above the garage door opening.

Side-hung: Definitely the oldest door style and requires the most space to operate.

COLOUR

Garage doors can be purchased in a fairly wide range of colours. If you cannot find a colour you like, then many of the doors will be available in a primer finish ready to receive a finishing coat. Doors are available with laminate, vinyl and powder coatings in a limited range of colours, with little maintenance required and a fairly lengthy manufacturer's guarantee.

INSTALLING THE GARAGE DOOR

Having selected the door most suitable for your needs, you must decide how it is to operate within the garage area. Where opening width is at a premium you may find it better to fit the door guides/runner/frame on the inside of the garage door opening, thus maximizing width. Where door-opening width is not a problem, fit the guides/runner/frame against the door-opening jambs.

It is important at this stage to ensure that all the fittings ready to receive the new door are level and square; this will ensure the door operates and performs properly. If the frame is not square the door will not open and close properly, and if it is not level the springs will not perform as well as they should.

The installation of a new garage door is not always considered to be a job for the inexperienced, but with more do-it-yourself outlets supplying ready-to-fix doors, the job has certainly become considerably easier. Garage doors are difficult to man-handle by one person, so organize assistance when necessary.

The area around the garage door opening should be cleared of all obstructions, and if this is the only access point into the garage, any items likely to be required during fitting should be made accessible.

Where the door is being fitted to a new timber frame, then follow the manufacturer's instructions.

The natural beauty of wooden side-hung garage doors.

Sectional overhead garage door.

If the new door is being fitted into runners, whether they are situated against the vertical jambs or inside them, make sure the runners are both square and level to ensure proper working and operating conditions. Always follow the manufacturer's installation instructions when fitting the door and runners.

AUTOMATIC REMOTE CONTROL

Automatic garage door-opening gear can be fitted to almost all vertically opening doors, and also to side-hung doors, although the process is a little more difficult. An electrical supply will need to be fitted close to where the door operating motor is to be fixed, and will normally require a 13amp supply fitted by an electrician.

Remote-controlled garage doors can be operated some distance from the garage by using a hand-held remote control, and most units have safety measures built in to avoid accidents. These will include an overload cutout when the door is jammed, and a reversing system when the door touches an obstruction. Be sure the remote control is tuned in to the correct wavelength and is not opening other doors in the area.

Step by Step

- Decide which door function works best within the space available, up and over or side opening.
- With such a wide range of materials and colours available you will need to decide which suits you and your home and your location best.
- Having selected the garage door, you will have to choose whether a garage door frame is required, and where the frame or runners are to be fitted.
- Although garage doors are designed to be easy to open and close manually, more and more people are installing electrical operating systems; make sure the electricity supply is fitted by an electrician and is in the correct place.
- When the door is fitted, if it is a 'primed' galvanized steel door it will need to be painted using a suitable paint.
- For garage doors to operate properly and continually the mechanisms should be well maintained. Do not use grease because this can attract gritty particles that will eventually damage the mechanism.

CHAPTER 10

Portable and Oak-Framed Garages

PORTABLE GARAGES

For several decades portable garage manufacturers have provided an ever-improving and increasing range of designs to meet the need for a state-of-the-art, weatherproof solution to vehicle storage and protection that doesn't cost a fortune. A comprehensive range of styles, sizes and shapes, in both traditional and modern designs, is currently available through a large number of experienced suppliers, all produced using only the highest quality materials.

The benefits or differences between erecting a portable garage and a permanent one are many and varied. The one feature shared in equal measure is the base upon which the garage is

Compton garage with a brick finish.

built: a secure, level concrete base is recommended, and any guarantees provided by the garage manufacturers will depend upon how well the base is laid and how level it is. The quality of the base may also determine how well the new garage works, and what maintenance is required during its lifetime.

With a variety of roof styles and wall finishes to choose from, the appearance of the new garage can be selected from the wide range available. Single and double doors can be fitted, along with windows and entrance doors. The majority of manufacturers will provide a 'supply and build' service on the base you have built.

Planning Permission

Building regulations approval is required for a garage with a floor area exceeding 30 square metres; most portable garages are therefore exempt from this requirement. A garage that is to be built along or behind the building line, and which does not project in front of the existing property, is similarly exempt. If you are not sure whether planning permission is required, seek advice from your local authority planning department. Although approval may not be required, it is important to make every effort to achieve good working conditions.

The Foundations

The site area must be cleared of all topsoil and any vegetative materials before the concrete slab is laid. It is unlikely that general foundations similar to those used in domestic construction

Flat-roofed Compton garage.

works for home extensions will be required, but when the area for the concrete base is cleared, extra excavations around the edges where the garage walls will be should be carried out. This will allow for a thicker concrete depth to support the extra weight of the walls, and it is vital that this part of the project is carried out diligently and expertly to avoid problems later on.

The concrete slab can be reinforced using reinforcing sheets where the weight imposed upon it is likely to be high.

The Walls

The walls of a portable garage interlock and will be of pre-cast concrete; if you are working on your own, you will need someone to help you. Each section is bolted to the one adjacent to it using rust-resistant fittings. External joints must be sealed according to the manufacturer's specifications, and must meet fire prevention regulations.

The Roof

Both flat and sloping roofs are available from manufacturers, and these must also comply with the necessary fire regulations. Flat roof slabs should be maintenance free. Pitched roofs will have timber or steel trusses, and there is a wide range of roof coverings to meet every need.

The Doors

The portable garage will be fitted with standard up-and-over doors in both timber and steel with galvanized steel frames. It is likely that the doors will require painting or treating as appropriate. Single and double garage doors are available within the range, along with a number of door designs. Personal doors providing an alternative access to the garage are also available.

Portable garage with a very attractive brick finish.

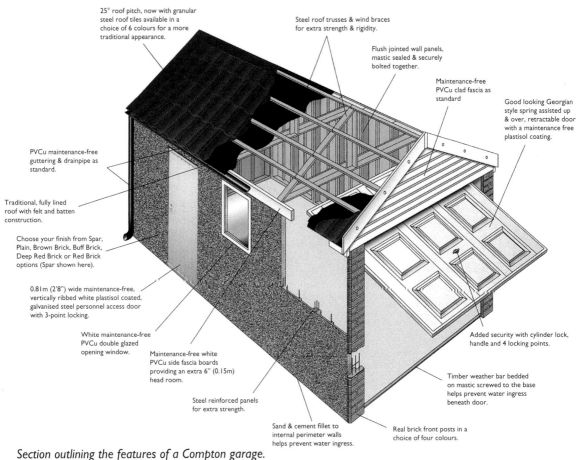

25° roof pitch, now with granular steel roof tiles available in a choice of 6 colours for a more traditional appearance.

Steel roof trusses & wind braces for extra strength & rigidity.

Flush jointed wall panels, mastic sealed & securely bolted together.

Maintenance-free PVCu clad fascia as standard

Good looking Georgian style spring assisted up & over, retractable door with a maintenance free plastisol coating.

PVCu maintenance-free guttering & drainpipe as standard.

Traditional, fully lined roof with felt and batten construction.

Choose your finish from Spar, Plain, Brown Brick, Buff Brick, Deep Red Brick or Red Brick options (Spar shown here).

0.81m (2'8") wide maintenance-free, vertically ribbed white plastisol coated, galvanised steel personnel access door with 3-point locking.

White maintenance-free PVCu double glazed opening window.

Maintenance-free white PVCu side fascia boards providing an extra 6" (0.15m) head room.

Steel reinforced panels for extra strength.

Sand & cement fillet to internal perimeter walls helps prevent water ingress.

Added security with cylinder lock, handle and 4 locking points.

Timber weather bar bedded on mastic screwed to the base helps prevent water ingress beneath door.

Real brick front posts in a choice of four colours.

Section outlining the features of a Compton garage.

Compton double garage.

OAK-FRAMED GARAGES

Oak has been used as a traditional building material for centuries, and it has truly passed the test of time. Magnificent purpose-built oak-framed garages built from sustainable woodland are now available in an extensive range that will meet almost every need. The use of home-grown 'green' building materials, and centuries-old carpentry skills together with the benefit of modern

Oakmasters double garage.

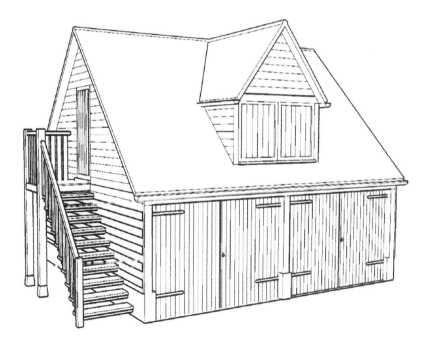

Typical oak-framed building.

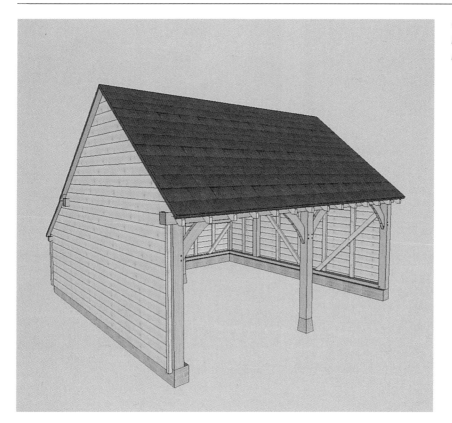

Oak-framed building: it can be bespoke or modular.

Oak-framed double garage with a room over.

A two-car garage.

techniques learned over many years, produces an end result of elegance and beauty with the potential for a very long life.

These garages are available in various shapes and sizes; they can also be built from personal designs and to suit personal requirements. They can be hand made or modular, and manufacturers can supply and fit them, or provide them as a kit to be assembled following building assembly instructions. They can be linked to adjacent buildings, and can be open fronted or securely enclosed. Log stores, stables and even a home office can be added to form the complete package.

Where an oak-framed garage is to be built off a base already completed, make sure the base is suitable for the purpose. The supplier will expect the base to be level and secure, and of a size suitable to meet their requirements. Should a base not be suitable when the supplier arrives to install the garage, further costs may incur.

Oak-framed garages plus store.

The range of possibilities with oak-framed garages is almost endless, and the end result is a building of true quality and character, extremely pleasing to the eye and eminently practical.

Oakmasters triple garage.

Inspection Pits and Driveways

INSTALLING AN INSPECTION PIT

A garage is clearly a place where you store your vehicle; it is also likely to be the place where you repair, service and work on it. To carry out this work safely and in more comfort than simply lying on the floor underneath your vehicle, an inspection pit is ideal. Anyone familiar with motor vehicle repairs will recognize the benefits of a 'pit'; however, there are other points that must be considered apart from its dimensions.

One of the most significant problems arising from an inspection pit is water. If the water table in your area is high, then extra precautions must be taken during construction, and how the land lies is also important. Rainwater may soak away well, but precautions must be taken to ensure it does not flow towards the pit area.

When these points have been considered and any problems resolved, then the type of inspection pit must be considered. Pits can be constructed in brickwork or blockwork off a proper foundation, though efforts should be made to waterproof the area. Of course, installing waterproof protection to keep water out will also, when it works well, keep water in, so some form of drainage by way of a sump should be considered. All these points are dependent upon the existing water table.

An alternative to brick or block construction is fibreglass. Pre-formed pits are available and easy to install providing you follow the manufacturer's instructions.

An inspection pit should be built at a width

Regulations for the Inspection Pit

Planning permission is only required where the inspection pit is to be installed in a listed building. However, to comply with building regulations you must observe the following conditions:

- Excavations should not affect the integrity of the garage foundations.
- No automotive fluids or spillages should be able to enter the watercourse.
- Electrical installations must comply with current regulations and be installed by an approved installer.

---

suitable for repair activities to be carried out, but not too wide to make parking the vehicle difficult or risky. However, it is important to ensure that there is enough room to work around the perimeter of the vehicle without affecting the pit area; for example, there should be enough room for a car jack so you can change a wheel.

Lighting should be installed, and will be necessary in what will be a very dark area. A qualified electrician should always be employed to ensure the correct current is used, and that both the cables and fittings meet the safety requirements necessary, and an 'earth' is provided if required.

Installing an inspection pit in a new garage will be a lot easier than installing one in a garage already built. The excavation works can be carried out at the same time as all the other

A pre-formed inspection pit in service.

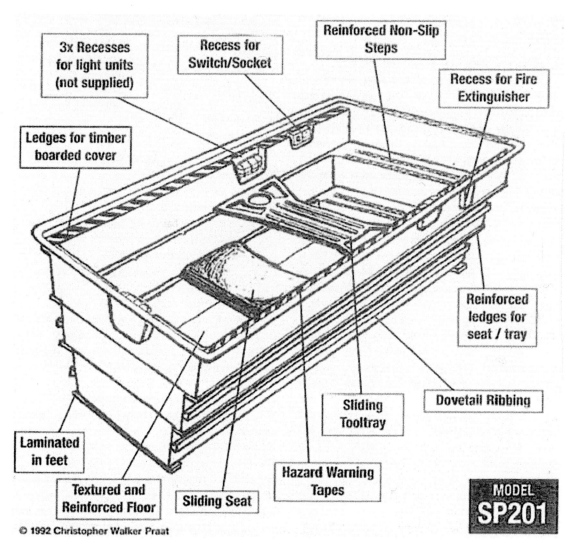

3x Recesses
for light units
(not supplied)

Recess for
Switch/Socket

Reinforced Non-Slip
Steps

Recess for Fire
Extinguisher

Ledges for timber
boarded cover

Reinforced
ledges for
seat / tray

Sliding
Tooltray

Dovetail Ribbing

Laminated
in feet

Hazard Warning
Tapes

MODEL
SP201

Textured and
Reinforced Floor

Sliding Seat

© 1992 Christopher Walker Praat

Inspection pit diagram.

excavation works, and all waste materials disposed of suitably.

CONSTRUCTING A DRIVEWAY

Access to the new garage must be considered during the planning process: after all, what use is a garage with no way for a vehicle to get in? Without any clear access route at planning stage, the planning committee will be concerned that the new building is to be used for something other than the storage of a vehicle – notwithstanding the knowledge that most existing garages are not used for the purpose they were designed for.

Strange though it may seem, building a garage may not attract the attention of the local authority planners, but building a driveway is a different matter, so much so that new legislation is currently in place to cover this very subject. This legislation has been introduced as a direct result of the effect that driveways, among other non-permeable landcover items including car parks, have had in adding substantially to the existing demands placed upon local land drainage systems. Flooding has been a high profile news item of late, and the effect of rainwater escaping to some areas has been devastating.

Planning Permission

If you are planning to construct a new driveway of more than 5 square metres and it is to be constructed with a non-permeable material, then you will need planning permission (as of 1 October 2008). Non-permeable materials include concrete, concrete slabs and tarmac, and any other non-porous material or materials. On the other hand, if you are planning to construct the new driveway using permeable materials, where water can drain through into the subsoil and disperse easily, then you will not need planning permission. Suitable permeable materials include gravel and shingle.

The Non-Permeable Driveway

A non-permeable driveway should always be laid on a solid and stable foundation. Simply laying a rigid surface of concrete, tarmac or paviors on top of a subsoil stripped of topsoil will almost inevitably lead to a number of problems, not least subsidence and cracking.

The area selected should be marked out properly as according to the plans, and the topsoil and subsoil removed to a minimum depth of 150mm. The topsoil can be set aside to be reused elsewhere in the garden. The remaining subsoil base will then need to achieve, at the very minimum, a regular and even rigidity. Building regulations do not cover the laying or construction of driveways, so a great deal of common sense will be needed. Preparations along the lines of the laying of an oversite concrete base for a new building will prove adequate, while bearing in mind the additional weightload that will be placed on the driveway in selective areas. The wheelstrips where cars, vans and lorries drive will always be under the greatest pressure, and any weaknesses will eventually be found out, so extra support in these areas will not be wasted.

When the whole area has been stripped of topsoil and sufficient subsoil to provide a stable area to work off, a base layer should be laid of scalpings or similar base material, as recommended to you by the local quarry. Calculate how much you require, and spread it over the area evenly. This base should be well compacted using a compaction machine before the finishing material is laid down.

Concrete and Tarmac Driveways

Concrete and tarmac are very consistent and reliable products that for many years have been used successfully to cover driveways, paths and roads; however, there are knock-on effects created by their non-porosity. I have covered the effect these materials can have on land drainage, and the effect of rainwater runoff over-working the local storm drainage systems, but there is another aspect of these materials that has an effect on global warming, which receives far less publicity. Basically, the heat from the sun is stored for long periods within these particular surfaces, and this forms a 'micro-climate' in and around large housing and industrial estates. More and more countries are now recognizing the effect these surfaces have when laid in large areas, and are endeavouring to deal with these issues by pushing for a more eco-friendly and 'greener' attitude.

The Eco-Friendly 'Green' Driveway

With so much anxiety concerning the climate changing and the planet warming, there is a genuine incentive to at least try to defer the effects of this phenomenon. From the practical point of view, an eco-friendly driveway should be easy to install and visually attractive, and it can also be very cost effective, though it is likely to demand regular maintenance.

An eco driveway can be constructed using driveway honeycomb grids constructed from recycled plastic with the cells filled with a mixture of sand and soil. The area is then seeded and treated as a standard lawn. The driveway grids must be laid on a firm, compressed soil bed to ensure even wear and to reduce the risk of constant vehicle use making ruts in the ground.

A typical profile of the Bodpave eco-driveway. (Courtesy Boddingtons Ltd)

Wheeltracks Only

The ultimate 'green' driveway is simply a row of bricks, blocks, slabs or shingle laid where the wheeltracks are to be. The areas between and on either side will be grass, or planted accordingly. This, as with the eco-friendly driveway, will allow surface water to drain off naturally, and will not be anywhere near as heat retentive as a full tarmac or concrete driveway.

Constructing a Turning Space

Leaving and entering a highway by motor vehicle is an action monitored closely by the local highways department. Where the road is likely to be busy, you will be notified to provide a turning space within your boundary, where a motor vehicle can turn round without endangering other road users. The turning space can be directly in front of the new garage or at least fairly adjacent to it.

Alterations to the Highway

Access to the site may already be in place, but where it isn't you will need approval from your local authority highways department, and must therefore submit a plan showing the existing site access and the surrounding areas, as well as a plan showing any alterations, such as dropping the kerb, that will be required. The highways department may require the work to be carried out by an approved contractor, especially where there is a pavement or pathway used by pedestrians.

Any work involving the excavation of roads or pathways must be undertaken with the full approval of the local council, and extra care should be taken to avoid services – electricity, gas, water – accessing the site.

An eco-driveway in action.

Paving grids can be used for grass or shingle.

A paving grid shingle driveway.

Step by Step

- Before excavating or laying out your driveway, check with the local authority regarding any local drainage issues, and the sustainable urban drainage system (SUDS).
- If you are laying a concrete or tarmac driveway, remove all topsoil and any plants and vegetative material.
- Make sure the driveway base is well rolled and secure for the purpose.
- Contact your local highways department before dropping the kerb or forming an access.
- Check where the incoming services such as electricity and gas are on site, and their locations in comparison to the new driveway.
- A turning space where a motor can turn round on site and not be required to reverse back on to the highway may be requested by the highways department or the planning department.

Useful Addresses

This short list of manufacturers and stockists has been prepared to help and guide you during the planning process and building of your new garage. If you have any questions regarding the products they offer I am sure they will be only too happy to answer your questions and supply you with any information you require.

I would also like to take this opportunity to thank them for the help they have given me during the production of this book.

Concrete Blocks:
Tarmac Topblock
Wolverhampton
(0845) 606 2468

Insulation Blocks:
Thermalite
Hanson Aggregates
(01628) 774100

Roof Tiles:
Marley Eternit
Burton upon Trent
(01253) 722588

Compton Garages:
Southam, Warks
(01293) 770291

Oak-Framed Garages:
Oakmasters
Hayward's Heath
West Sussex
RH16 4RZ
(01444) 455455

Garage Doors:
Gliderol Roller Doors
County Durham
(0191) 5180455

Henderson Garage Doors
Luton
(0844) 4632351

Eco Driveways:
Boddingtons
Essex
(01621) 874299

Inspection Pits:

www.mech-mate.co.uk
(01923) 265500

Crown Oak Buildings
Kent
(01732) 866910

Index